BUD

THE BRANDO
I KNEW

The Untold Story of Brando's Private Life

CARLO FIORE

DELACORTE PRESS / NEW YORK

Designed by Joel Schick

Manufactured in the United States of America
First printing

LIBRARY OF CONGRESS CATALOGING IN PUBLICATION DATA
Fiore, Carlo, 1919-
Bud: the Brando I knew.
1. Brando, Marlon.   I. Title.
PN2287.B683F5   791.43'028'0924   73-18286

ISBN: 0-440-01815-3

For Marcia

170841

Rashness, when it fails, is called madness.
When it succeeds, it is called genius.

—ANON.

BUD: THE BRANDO I KNEW

CHAPTER ONE

I MET MARLON BRANDO in 1944 when he was a callow twenty-year-old, and although he already displayed some talent as an actor, I wondered whether he would ever make it. Certainly I never thought my new friend would become one of the most celebrated actors of his time. He seemed much too easygoing and undisciplined to succeed at anything. Marlon didn't foresee his future success either. Years later, after he got an Academy Award for his performance in *On the Waterfront*, I asked him if he had any inkling during those early years that someday he might win an Oscar.

"How could anybody have guessed?" he said. "I feel as

though a skyhook caught me at the scruff of the neck and zoomed me straight up."

We met as fellow beginning actors in Erwin Piscator's Dramatic Workshop in the New School for Social Research in New York. Piscator was one of the most exciting men in the New York theater. He had worked with that great theatrical innovator and master of spectacle, Max Reinhardt, and then had struck out on his own to create the famous Epic Theater in Germany. But Hitler was in power, and because Piscator had married a Jewish ballet dancer, Maria Ley, and opposed the Fuehrer on principle, the dictator ordered his arrest. Fortunately for Piscator, the SS arrested the wrong man, and he escaped with his wife to the United States. In New York he formed his theatrical group, the Dramatic Workshop, at the New School.

Marlon had been studying at the Workshop about a year before I met him and was the favorite pupil of Stella Adler, who taught there. I had heard much about him. Broadway critics didn't normally cover student productions, but they came to see the shows at the New School because of Piscator's formidable reputation as an avant-garde producer. They wrote rave reviews of Marlon's performances, confirming the opinion of Miss Adler, who predicted, "One day this puppy thing will become America's finest actor."

When Piscator announced that he needed a "character actor" to complete his company and would hold auditions at the New School, every young actor in New York took notice. The winner of the audition would begin immediately as a member of the troupe the director was taking to the summer theater in Sayville, Long Island, for a season of repertory.

I was among the hopefuls who swarmed down to Twelfth Street in response to this call—as unlikely a prospect to win the contest as anyone could imagine. Born of immigrant Sicilian parents, I had left high school after a year and gone to work in a factory, steam-pressing men's garments. I wore my hair in a slick pompadour, combed in a ducktail at the neck. I wore the zoot suits that were the fad of the time, and blue suede shoes. My speech was unmistakably Brooklynese. But I had sense enough to try to make these shortcomings work for rather than against me.

Auditioning for Piscator, however, might never have entered my mind if I hadn't encountered on Sixth Avenue another actor I knew. Since he was usually as unadorned as the lofts he acted and lived in, I was surprised to see him dressed up. When I remarked about it, he told me, "They're holding auditions for the Dramatic Workshop," and hurried off.

I was brash and eager enough to follow him, meanwhile making up my mind what I would do for the great Piscator. I knew that I would be acceptable as an actor only if I portrayed a character who physically resembled me and was like me in manner and speech. So I chose a scene from *The Last Mile*, playing a meter reader who had been tried and convicted for the murder of a sixteen-year-old girl. In the scene a group of reporters interview him through the bars of his cell on Death Row, and because he did not take the stand in his defense during the trial, it is his first opportunity to tell the world his side of the story.

When I climbed the steps to the stage in the New School auditorium, my knees almost buckled. My voice was shaky, and my mouth was so dry that my tongue stuck to my palate. Somehow I managed to get through the scene.

After I finished, I heard Piscator thanking me from the semi-darkness of the auditorium, after which he got up and left. I thought I had been dismissed and was making my way to the wings when the director's assistant, Chouteau Dyer, an efficient, schoolteacherish woman of thirty or so, came up and handed me a railway ticket. She instructed me to pack for a twelve-week stay in summer stock and told me to meet with the rest of the company at Penn Station at precisely eight o'clock next morning. Then she turned away abruptly and walked off.

I had won, and I was dumfounded. If I hadn't had the tangible evidence of the railway ticket in my hand, I would have believed the whole thing was a dream.

Next morning at eight, dressed in my best zoot suit and suede shoes, hair lacquered in place like a helmet, I arrived in the Long Island terminal on the lower level of Penn Station, lugging an enormous cheap suitcase crammed with everything I owned in the world. Miss Dyer and the company were standing in a group at one of the gates, and I joined them. I was introduced to a dozen or more students. They welcomed me politely, but since I was a stranger, shy and silent, they quickly ignored me, turned to their friends and picked up conversations where they had left off. Only one took much notice of me. A tall, slim, vivacious blonde whose name was Elaine Stritch did a quick double-take when she saw my strange costume and exclaimed, "Are you a gangster? I hope so. I simply *adore* gangsters!"

Marlon Brando was the last to arrive. He was carrying two leather bags which looked very expensive to me, and he was wearing a button-down Oxford shirt open at the neck, tan cotton slacks, and scuffed tennis shoes. He was the image of the ideal American youth—dark blond hair, blue-gray eyes, tawny complexion, a stride that was an easy athletic lope. The map of the United States was etched on his features.

On the train, I sat apart from the others and watched the landscape sliding by through my reflection in the window, listening enviously to the chatter and laughter of the company sitting behind me at the rear of the car.

Somebody said "Hi," and when I looked up, Marlon was standing in the aisle. He sat down beside me, introduced himself, and we shook hands.

"Being exclusive?" he asked, smiling.

"No," I replied.

"Are you shy?"

"A little."

"Everybody's shy at the beginning. You'll get over it in a few minutes. Come on, join us. You've got to break the ice sometime. It might as well be now."

"Not now. Not yet," I said. "They're having a lot of fun and a stranger might put a damper on it."

"Right," he said. "I know what you mean." He got up to go. "See you later."

"Thank you," I said. "Thank you very much."

"Right," he said, grinning, and walked down the aisle to join his friends.

That was all, and I stayed aloof until we got off the train in Sayville and saw the theater for the first time. I remember it as one of the most beautiful theaters I had seen. It was situated on a bay of dazzling blue, and its terrace bordered a private beach of bone-white sand. Broad expanses of meadows overgrown with tall grass, weeds, and wildflowers surrounded it. A wide country lane meandered for about a mile from the theater through the fields to a small, quiet town. The exterior of the theater was white Colonial, and it looked as though it might have been an inn a century before; but when we entered, there was a breath-taking, splendid, full-sized theater.

Everyone was excited at the prospect of spending a summer in such magnificent surroundings. We were eager to settle in, explore the grounds, and perhaps have a swim in the bay before dinner, but we hadn't been given any instructions and

The theater in Sayville with cast members in costumes and bathing suits. (KARGER-PIX FOR Collier's)

didn't know what to do. Restlessly, we stood around on stage with our luggage at our feet, waiting to be shown to our living quarters.

Miss Dyer, who had disappeared for a while, finally returned and announced, with the authoritative voice of someone thoroughly familiar with the building's layout, "All right, children, here are your instructions. And please listen carefully because I don't intend to repeat them. You will sleep, eat, and work in this building. We want you *here. All* of you *here*, so that we can keep an eye on you. Now, then, after you get these instructions, you will pick up your luggage and hunt for a place to flop. And I mean *flop*. So don't be too choosy. Take what you can get, or you may find yourself sleeping in the kitchen. When you find a room, a dressing room, or whatever, you may claim that space as your own by placing your luggage on the spot. There aren't enough rooms to accommodate everybody, so double up wherever you can. We didn't assign you to sleeping quarters because, in this way, you will have no one but yourselves to blame for what you get."

She pointed to double doors that were wide open at stage right. "You will find bed frames, bedding, and an odd assortment of furniture in that storeroom. Good luck!"

The company snapped up their luggage and scattered in every direction.

I didn't join the scramble to find a place to sleep, because I thought it would have appeared unseemly conduct on my part, to say the least. I was the only one in the company not paying tuition, and I was getting my bed and board gratis. Being there at all was a fluke, I thought, and I felt glad to have any sleeping space that might be available.

I saw Marlon approach, minus his luggage, so I figured he was all set up.

"Find a place?" he asked me.

"No," I said. "Not yet."

"Do you snore?"

"Huh?"

"I said, do you snore?"

"I don't think so. No."

"Want to bunk with me?"

"Yeah. Sure," I said.

"Well, then, follow me."

I stooped to hoist my suitcase onto my shoulder.

"Better leave that here," he said. "We'll come back for it later."

I gave him a look full of doubt. Everything I owned was contained in that suitcase.

Marlon smiled broadly. "Nobody's going to steal it. Come on, let's hurry, before somebody jumps my claim."

He led me to a dismantled double bed and a dilapidated wooden dresser, which he had somehow managed to move outside the theater. We picked up the mattress and carried it across the meadow toward an old, weatherbeaten barn. The dirt floor within the barn sprouted weeds up to the hips. Rusted farming tools and a couple of bald truck tires were scattered about. A rickety ladder slanted upward to a trap door in the wooden ceiling. We lugged the mattress up the ladder, wrestled it through the trap door, and landed in a rather clean, bare attic. Two large windows at opposite ends made the room bright and airy.

"Well, what do you think?" Marlon asked, making a sweeping gesture with his arm.

"Not bad," I said. "Not bad at all."

"It's perfect. Come here. Look."

I joined him at the window and saw a marvelous view of the theater and the bay.

"From this window," he said, "we can see anybody approaching from the theater." He turned and walked to the window at the opposite end. I followed. "And from this window we can spot anybody coming up the road from town. And if we don't want to see anybody we can pull up the ladder. There will be times when we'll want privacy. Complete privacy. By the way, one of the girls has already buzzed me about you. She thinks you're sexy."

"Oh?" I said, inwardly perking up, but feigning only a mild interest. "Which one?"

"Esther. The little blonde with the big boobs."

"Oh," I said, instantly deflated. Esther was the plainest girl in the company.

"What's the matter?" Marlon said. "Don't you prefer girls with big boobs?"

"Not particularly," I said.

[8]

"Neither do I. Let's get the rest of our stuff. We can talk later."

We stepped down through the trap door and descended the ladder to retrieve my suitcase.

By the time we got to bed that night, I realized with great relief that I felt no uneasiness in sharing a bed with someone who had been a total stranger until that morning. We were instant friends. Stimulated by all the events of that day and our new surroundings, we lay awake and talked all night. Finally, with the first daylight, Marlon's eyelids began to droop, and soon he slipped off into a sound sleep.

I turned on my side with my back to him, puffed up my pillow, settled my head on it, and just as I was about to doze off, Marlon snored. Deep snores, rumbling like distant thunder, and powerful. If there had been curtains on the windows, they would have snapped like flags in the stiff breeze.

So began our first summer.

CHAPTER TWO

LIFE WAS PLEASANT. When we weren't rehearsing, we went swimming in the bay, or walked through the meadows. Marlon borrowed a convertible and we drove around a lot, often stopping to eat at some restaurant. My new friend ate a lot, but he was no gourmet. He liked quick food, like a child—hamburgers, hot dogs, French fries, thick malteds. Later, when he could afford to eat in the best restaurants and I was eager to satisfy my own taste for good French cuisine, Marlon invariably would pick out the cheapest joints.

In the theater, he never appeared to be working at all. He

never knew his lines and often failed to pick up his cues. He kept the play script handy backstage so he wouldn't get totally lost. The truth was that Marlon hadn't really decided to be an actor, and until he made that decision during *Truckline Cafe*, his second Broadway appearance, his approach to acting was completely undisciplined.

Not long after the season began, his mother came to visit him, and the three of us went out to dinner. She was a true beauty, tall, willowy, ash-blonde, with large wide-set eyes appearing constantly to change color, reflecting hazel or gray and sometimes green, depending on the light. She was soft-spoken, and she had rare style. Her name was Dorothy Pennebaker Brando, but from the very beginning she insisted I call her Dodie.

The waiter asked us if we wanted a drink before dinner. Dodie and Marlon shook their heads. I ordered a martini. I didn't like drinking alone very much, and Dodie sensed it.

"I'm sorry about your having to drink alone," she said. "I'd like to join you, but I can't. I'm an alcoholic. You know—one drink is too many, one thousand not enough."

This sudden confession jolted me. "In that case, I'll cancel the martini," I said.

"Please don't," Dodie said with a slight smile. "I get vicarious pleasure watching friends enjoy their drinks. You're not going to deny me that, are you?"

I didn't know what to say, so I said nothing.

"I think I spoke too soon," she went on. "I'm sorry. I should have waited until you had had your martini. I hate for you to think that I instantly confess my little problem to all and sundry. But Bud told me that you two have become close friends, and I wanted you to hear it from me, not from anybody else."

[11]

*Marlon and colleagues
drumming up trade for
the summer theater.*
(KARGER-PIX FOR Collier's)

That was the first time I had heard Marlon called by his family nickname, Bud. But later, when I attempted to use it, he would have none of it. "My name is Marlon," he said firmly. "Bud belongs back home." I was using my professional name then, Frederick Stevens, and when Brando began calling me Freddie, I tried to retaliate, saying just as firmly, "Don't call me Freddie. My name is Carlo." But Marlon would have none of that either. He simply ignored my protest, and I was always Freddie to him.

Dodie and Marlon and I sat quietly listening to the music while I sipped my martini. A trio—piano, bass, and tenor sax —was playing "Blue Moon," and several couples got up to dance.

"Will you dance with me?" Dodie asked.

"My pleasure," I said.

We got up, made our way to the dancing area, and glided smoothly across the polished hardwood floor. I caught a glimpse of Marlon, elbows on the table, chin cupped in his hands, staring at me with unblinking, blank eyes, and I was afraid he was reading my mind, which must have been as easy to read as an open book. I blushed scarlet. It has always been impossible for me to disguise a strong desire for a woman, especially if I was dancing with her, and at that moment there was nothing I wanted more in the world than to make love to Marlon's beautiful mother. That desire was stimulated when she placed her pelvis close against me as we danced. I couldn't help getting an erection when she brushed her thigh against me as we moved.

Mercifully, the set ended. We didn't dance again, and after dinner was over we accompanied Dodie to the rooms she had rented, said good night to her, and Marlon and I continued on toward the theater.

It was a warm, starry, moon-bright night in June, and as we walked we talked about women. Marlon appeared distressed when I confessed that once in a while I got a terrific yen for older women. For a time we walked side by side in silence, until Marlon turned, fixed me with a penetrating stare, and inquired suddenly, "Would you go to bed with my mother?"

I looked at him and wondered if he was playing one of his favorite games. He loved to shock you, then study your reaction. But I saw it was no game this time. He was deadly serious. I have always been an inept liar, and to deny that I was sexually attracted to Dodie would have been a lie, and Marlon would have seen right through it. There was no way I could hedge the question, and his anguished expression told me that a great deal depended on my answer.

"Well, would you?" he insisted.

"No," I said. "Never."

"Why not? You just told me that you liked older women. Suppose Dodie made herself . . . available. Suppose she wanted to. Why not?"

"Because you're my friend. I wouldn't hurt your feelings like that."

He looked into my eyes for a second or two, searching for the lie, then he gave me a curt nod, as if to say he believed me, and that was the end of it.

Suddenly his face cracked with a cockeyed grin, and he burst out laughing, leaving me confused again. Maybe he *was* playing the game, and I was taken in again. But I was beginning to understand him now. These lunatic about-face reactions in moments of crisis were his way of coping with his embarrassment, a method he used to ease the tension.

"Come on. I'll race you to the barn," Marlon said, jogging in place, loosening his muscles.

"I don't feel like running," I said.

"Oh, come on. The exercise will do you good."

"No," I said firmly.

"I'll give you a head start. I'll run halfway backward."

"I said *no*, and I mean *no*."

He sank a stiff left hook in my solar plexus that knocked the wind out of me and almost doubled me up. When I recovered from the shock of the unexpected blow, Marlon was kicking up dust racing toward the barn. I was in a rage and wanted to fight him, to knock his block off if I could. But he had a long lead on me, and I knew I'd never catch him. I walked toward the barn, taking my time and plotting revenge.

I hadn't lied to him about Dodie. Much as I wanted to sleep with her, I wouldn't have, and later in our relationship I had the chance to prove it, when she gave me the plain invitation and I refused.

"Why not?" she asked. "Because of my son?"

"Yes," I said. "That's it."

She nodded and said nothing more.

Later, in my night conversations with Marlon, when we often talked for hours and I got to know more about his early family life back in Nebraska, I found out why he had asked me that question after he had watched me dancing with Dodie. When he was young, back home, and his mother was already alcoholic, he would sometimes be called to come down to a bar and get his mother and take her home. Once he had found her drunk with a Marine, and when he tried to pry her away, they had both told him to get lost. He was crushed. Marlon hadn't liked his father either, I discovered. His father had been a traveling salesman and, as Marlon told it, often came in from the road with lipstick on his shirts and shorts, and he could hear father and mother quarreling about it in their bedroom and Dodie screaming, "At least you could get your laundry done and I wouldn't have to see it." That might have been Marlon's fantasy, conditioned by his deep feeling for his mother. I don't know.

Sometimes these family quarrels ended with his father beating up his mother, and Marlon told me that when he was about thirteen or fourteen he had told his father that if he ever touched Dodie again, he would kill him. That may have been early dramatics too. His sister Jocelyn, who at the time Marlon and I met was already an actress in New York, told me that he was always making dramatic gestures, like clutching his heart and pretending to fall to the floor in a faint, while he was growing up. Nevertheless, I could understand it when he told me that when his father died, many years later, he felt nothing at all.

Dodie had come to Sayville to see Marlon play in our first production, which took place the night after our dinner together. She would have done better to stay home. Our gala premiere was a disaster.

Fire Island vacationers had ferried across the bay to see us, and the exclusive sailing crowd in Sayville had surprised us by turning out in large numbers. We found ourselves playing to a house of sophisticated, seasoned theatergoers. The play was *Twelfth Night*, and Marlon played Sebastian, the young, romantic lead. I was cast as his friend Antonio, a pirate-sailor. Few of the actors had committed Shakespeare's verse firmly to memory, and instead of "performing," we were "reaching for lines." We were also a little confused about our exact positions on stage. Consequently what was intended to be a bawdy comedy was instead a depressing fiasco, and after three ghastly hours the audience and the exhausted cast were both enormously relieved to see the curtain come down.

The auditorium emptied rapidly, and Miss Dyer told the cast to remain on stage; Mr. Piscator wanted to speak to us. We sat wherever we could on the set, uncomfortable in our sweat-soggy costumes and blurred makeup, disgusted with ourselves, knowing well we deserved the dressing down that was sure to come.

Like children, we had taken advantage of the absence of authority. Piscator had not been with us much during rehearsals because he had been commissioned to direct a new play for Broadway, and he had passed over the directing chores to his wife, Maria, a kind and gentle woman who was incapable of giving us the discipline we needed. So we had bathed bare-assed in the bay at night, held all-night bull

The author (with God-given nose) as sea captain rescuing Dorothy Spaulding, while Erwin Piscator directs Twelfth Night *rehearsal.*
(KARGER-PIX FOR Collier's)

sessions in the barn where we lived (it had been the company's hangout), read poetry, flirted, and made love—all of this when we should have been thinking about our roles and memorizing our lines.

Piscator had taken a day off to come out to Sayville so that he could give our play a final polish before opening night. The chaotic dress rehearsal he saw dismayed him. He knew it would take far more than the twenty-four hours available to get the play into shape. The cast knew it too, and we pleaded with him to postpone the opening for a few days. But he had flatly refused and walked out of the theater. Consequently we had opened on schedule, bombed as expected, and now we waited on stage with quiet resignation, like condemned criminals, to have our heads chopped off.

Even I, who had seen so little of Piscator, was apprehensive. He was a small, energetic man with iron-gray hair and piercing eyes of cobalt blue who spoke with a thick German accent. His temperament was normally gentle and mild, but he was widely known to have a terrible temper. When he arrived that night, however, intending to give us hell, and saw how remorseful and woebegone we were, he relented. Rather than dealing out punishment, he decided to give us some advice. He reminded us of the importance of self-discipline, hard work, and an actor's responsibility to his fellow actors. If that night's debacle had taught us that important lesson, once and for all, he would consider the evening a success. He called an early rehearsal for next day, told us to get some rest, and we dispersed silently.

The cast rehearsed well and hard next morning, and company morale was lifted to some degree. Lunch was laid out buffet-style on the terrace, and Marlon and I sat together. He picked at his food without appetite and seemed more depressed than ever.

"What's wrong?" I said. "Don't you like boiled pigs' knuckles?"

"Nope," he replied.

"Let's walk to town for a hamburger and malt," I said. "We've got time. Okay?"

"Okay," Marlon said without enthusiasm.

It was an extraordinarily lovely day. A cool breeze from the bay raced and rippled over the tall grass and wild flowers. But Marlon took no notice. He walked with his head lowered, hands in pockets, and occasionally kicked at a small stone in his path.

"Something bothering you?" I said.

"Dodie sailed into me this morning," he said.

"About last night's performance?"

"That and a thousand other things."

"She'll get over it," I said. "Mothers always do."

"She meant it this time. She left this morning. Told me not to call her until I decided to grow up."

I was sorry to hear she was gone. I knew she had planned to stay for a week, and I was looking forward to seeing her again.

"Grow up?" I said. "How . . . grow up?"

"She told me to take acting seriously or go into business with Pop."

"That sounds sensible," I said.

"Yeah, but she *knows* I'd never go into business with Pop."

"Why, what's he in?"

"He's with a chemical feed company. Cattle feed. Fattens steers for the market."

"What's wrong with that?"

"Nothing, if that's what you want to do. But I don't. And she knows it. This is the first time I've goofed off in a play, the first time, and she cuts out. Just like that."

Marlon and Blossom Plumb rehearsing for Twelfth Night. (KARGER-PIX FOR Collier's)

"Nobody likes a loser," I said. "Nobody."

"That's true," Marlon said. "Not even your own mother. But still . . ." He picked up a stone and angrily pitched it at the trunk of a tree. "Shit!"

He was disturbed, all right, but he seemed to get over it in the following weeks. Things went better after that disastrous opening night. Our plays began to attract a sizable patronage, and we played mostly to full houses. We were often invited to parties given in the homes of townspeople, and occasionally we went sailing in their boats on the bay.

Then, right in the middle of that idyllic summer, Marlon was expelled. Piscator was given to forays around the premises, and one afternoon during rest period he found Marlon and one of the girls (I'll call her Deborah) in the barn, in bed, asleep. We had been warned time and again that if any of us were caught in such a situation we would be sent home immediately. The decision would be irrevocable; no amount of pleading would reverse it. The director considered it unthinkable to have to send a daughter entrusted to his care back to her mother and father because she was pregnant.

Anxiously the company waited outside Piscator's office. We hoped that just this once he would ignore the breaking of his unbreakable rule. At last the office door opened. Piscator, Marlon, and Deborah emerged, the latter two with their eyes puffed and red from crying. We knew without being told that they had not been forgiven.

I helped Marlon pack. As we talked about what had happened, the irony of it began to overwhelm us. For one thing, we both knew that Deborah was still a virgin. They had been discovered *on* the bed but not *in* it, and they were fully clothed. They had been prompting each other in memorizing their dialogue, and in the quiet of the barn they had gotten sleepy and simply taken a nap. It was as innocent as that. If they had planned to have sex, Marlon would have taken the precaution of pulling up the ladder behind him, and he would have bolted the trap door.

For another thing, Marlon had been guilty, along with most of the others in the company, of screwing all over the place for weeks, but on this one occasion, when he had done nothing at all, he had been caught. I wondered what Piscator would have said if he had known about the night we gave shelter to a girl who had no place to sleep, for reasons that escape me now. Both of us wanted to screw her, and Marlon was perfectly willing to share. We all climbed into bed together, because there was no other choice, but the girl fancied herself in love with my friend and would have no one but him.

While he was humping away silently in the dark, and I was stretched out, frustrated, beside them, I felt Marlon reach out a hand and pass it over my face.

"What's the matter?" I said irritably. "What's that for?"

"I thought you were crying," my friend said softly.

Not only had there been a great deal of this casual screwing but there had been a period of impassioned, specific love-making when Marlon's first love, I'll call her Maria Lorca, came out from New York to visit him and renew the affair they had been carrying on in the city. She was a good-looking, high-fashion type, about thirty years old. Maria was so proud of being Spanish that she was constantly making sure you didn't think she was Mexican or Puerto Rican.

Marlon and Maria lived together after that summer in the Park Savoy, a little hotel on Fifty-eighth Street, off Seventh Avenue. As a man who was in a state of perpetual erection himself, he told me with amusement and appreciation what a sexual freak Maria was, how he would screw her dog-fashion while she was on the telephone, and at various other times and places in a countless variety of ways.

Maria was the first to illustrate a characteristic that seemed to be true of the girls who fell in love with Marlon and stayed with him for any length of time. He would cast them off and take on someone new, and they would disappear for a while, then years later they would turn up in his life again, sometimes even working for him, and without any evidence of rancor or recrimination. Psychologists might call that an ongoing relationship, but I'd say they just couldn't get him out of their systems, and Marlon would never let them really go.

After Marlon threw over Maria for Movita (more of her later), she turned up years later as his secretary. She was not a euphemistic "secretary" either; she had been working at that occupation when they lived together in New York. In Hollywood, she assiduously cultivated the good will of the important movie columnists, people like Hedda Hopper, Louella Parsons, and Dale Harrison, all of whom Marlon hated. Miss Hopper once wrote: "I don't know what Marlon Brando has done to deserve so good and devoted a companion as Maria Lorca."

Unfortunately for her, Maria undertook to run Marlon's life, particularly which people were permitted to see him. One of the friends she didn't like happened to be me. I remember one time Marlon wanted me for a dress-call, which I wanted very much because a "dress" extra got about double the usual pay for it.

"I'm not going, I can't do it," I had to tell Marlon. "I haven't got a tuxedo."

"That's no problem," Marlon said. "I'll lend you mine. We're the same height. Tell Maria to give you my tuxedo, and come on."

When I called Maria and asked her when I could pick up the suit, she put on her most upper-class voice and said, "Do you know that suit cost two hundred and fifty dollars?"

"I'll take good care of it," I said, "Marlon said I could borrow it."

"Well," she said doubtfully, "it's against my better judgment, but hold on a minute and I'll see if I can find it."

She was back on a few minutes later. "I've looked around, and I can't find it anywhere," she said.

By that time I was furious. "Bullshit!" I said succinctly and hung up.

Later that night Marlon came over, looking disturbed.

"Listen," he said, "you were rude to Maria and hung up on her."

"I'd have been ruder if she had been there," I said, and told him the whole story.

"Couldn't *find* it!" Marlon said softly when I was through. "But I've got *two*!" He shook his head.

Next day he scolded her, but he didn't fire her, even though my complaint about Maria was one of dozens he was getting from his friends. There were enough of these eventually so that he had no choice but to dismiss her. Years later when she became his secretary again, he had to fire her once more.

"This is the second time you've done this to me," she protested, but no doubt there would have been a third time if circumstances and time had brought them together again.

During that golden summer in Sayville, however, all this lay ahead for Maria, and for Brando she was only one, although at the moment the chief one, of the girls he was screwing that season.

After we packed Marlon's things, we exchanged farewells, clasped hands, and promised to keep in touch. From the window I saw him toss his bags into a waiting cab and wave good-bye to the company, assembled to see him off.

I sat quietly in our room for a while, thinking about the things we had done together and the things he had told me. I remembered that it wasn't the first time he had been expelled from a place. He told me that he had once been kicked out of a military academy—for smoking, I think, or for conduct unbecoming a gentleman, or some other breach of the academy's rigid regulations. Now, banished again from his friends, it didn't require a psychologist to speculate that this second shock to his adolescent psyche might well produce a hostility to the establishment. If anyone doubted it, Marlon would prove it later.

Marlon before he was expelled
from military school.

[25]

CHAPTER THREE

W E MISSED MARLON very
much. The Sayville Theater was not the same without him.
Days were all work, and the nights were no fun. Our old barn
was declared off limits as a result of the scandal, and I slept on
an army cot in a tiny, windowless cubicle. I plunged into
work and study and managed to plod through the season to
its end.

During those twelve weeks I learned that acting was a
tough, demanding profession that ruined the nerves and dis-
torted the ego. I also learned not to put all that goo in my
hair. I came to understand that only clowns wore zoot suits
and blue suede shoes and subsequently acquired a taste for

conservative clothes. By diligent work on my speech and diction, I had gotten rid of my Brooklyn accent.

There was only one more thing I needed for a career in the professional theater, I thought. I would have to have my nose straightened. Mrs. Piscator thought I was a fool to have the shape of my nose altered. She said I had a beautiful nose, a handsome, manly nose that was perfectly suited to my face.

"Please don't ruin it," she said. "Don't take that awful chance."

I wish I had listened to her.

Seven months and five operations later, with savings depleted, I finally had a nose that somewhat conformed to the contours of my face. It wasn't my old nose, but it was enough; it would serve.

In those seven months I had seen none of the new friends I had made in the theater at Sayville, and I longed to see them again, now that I had outgrown my old Brooklyn buddies. They seemed strange to me after the summer season, with their zoot suits and ducktail hair styles, taking their girls dancing at the Flatbush Roseland on Saturday night. My former girl friend had given me up and found somebody new. I was convinced our old sexual attraction could be rekindled if we saw each other again, and once or twice I thought about calling her, but decided not to. Her new boy friend might hear about it and come looking for me; after all, he was Sicilian too. No, I couldn't go home again, and I really didn't want to. My old corner in Brooklyn was gone.

Besides, it felt good to walk along the theater district in Manhattan, to drop in at the old Stage Delicatessen, and eat succulent slices of corned beef between slabs of fresh rye bread, washing it down with cold, sparkling celery tonic.

As I stepped out of the Stage one day, I heard my name

shouted from a distance and froze. My first impulse was to run and hide in a doorway, but I held my ground. I saw that it was Zachary Charles, an actor I knew who had been playing in a musical comedy on Broadway. He ran across the street to me and planted himself in my way.

"Where the hell have you been hiding?" he inquired, pumping my hand energetically. "Where did you disappear to?" He focused on my nose. "So you went ahead and had it done."

"I'm afraid so," I said.

"It's not bad," he said, scrutinizing it closely.

"Yeah," I said dully.

"No, really, it's not bad," he said. "I just think you put yourself through all that torture for nothing. The original was just as good."

"Better," I said.

"Say, Marlon keeps asking about you. He's in *I Remember Mama* at the Barrymore."

"Yes, I know."

"Let's visit him. He's staying with his mother on West End Avenue. Let's go. Okay?"

I was ashamed of my bobbed nose. I felt I had defiled myself, and every meeting with friends, new or old, was going to be painful to me, at least for a time. But when Zachary saw me hesitate, he put a firm grip on my elbow.

"Come on," he said, pulling me to the edge of the sidewalk. "I promised Marlon I'd take you to him if I saw you, even if I had to drag you. Taxi!"

When we got to the apartment on West End, there was a brief awkwardness about our reunion. Marlon and Dodie had lost their suntans and were noticeably thinner, but still they made an extremely good-looking pair. Then the awkwardness melted, and we were good friends again. With exquisite discretion, neither of them mentioned, or even seemed to notice, my new nose.

(Marlon didn't think much of the job, however. Years later, we were having dinner one night with Rita Moreno, and we got involved in a long argument in which I stubbornly refused to accept something Marlon was trying to prove. "What are you disagreeing about?" he exclaimed at last. "It's as plain as the nose that used to be on your face.")

It was late in the afternoon, and Zachary had to leave to keep another appointment. Dodie insisted I remain to have dinner with them in the apartment, and after dinner Marlon said, following her up, he wanted me to go with him to the theater and see him perform in *I Remember Mama*. I was happy to accept both invitations.

"Come with me," Dodie said, "so we can talk while I fix you a drink. Let's see—you like martinis. Am I right?"

"Yes," I said, flattered that she remembered.

I followed her to the kitchen and she opened a cupboard stocked with liquor. I watched her as she carefully put together the ingredients of a martini. As she poured the icy liquid into an oversized champagne glass, I noticed that her hand shook. It crossed my mind that having a shelf of liquor so readily available might be too great a temptation for her to resist.

"Drink up," she said with a slight, self-conscious smile. "Don't worry about me. I don't touch the stuff myself. I keep it for friends who drop in."

I wanted to believe her, but she lowered her eyes quickly, and I was filled with doubt.

We sat down to dinner and the maid served a thick, delicious lentil soup. Conversation always flowed smoothly and spontaneously with us, but suddenly there was a silence and the atmosphere became oddly tense.

Dodie rose from her chair. "Excuse me," she said. "Please go on without me. I'll only be a minute." She left the room.

Marlon put down his spoon, slumped in his seat, and stared at his soup.

"What's the matter?" I said.

"I think Dodie has started drinking again."

We had no time to talk about it then. Dodie returned, dinner went on smoothly, and we went to the theater soon after. On the way, we talked about the play.

At rehearsals, Marlon said, he had been amused by Oscar Homolka, the veteran actor, who always had his nose in the script. He walked about the stage, mumbling his lines, tapping an actor occasionally and saying, "You will be here, huh?" never lifting his head. Marlon didn't go that far, but then or later he never tried to act during rehearsals. He simply walked through his roles, always registering keenly in his mind what he should be feeling and doing when it came time for the audience to see him.

That night when the final curtain came down, I went backstage to Marlon's dressing room. The play was a smash, and there was a crowd of well-wishers hanging around. Marlon was signing autographs, which was something he hated to do. When he saw me, he extricated himself quickly and we hurried out to the street.

In the taxi going uptown, he asked, "Well, what do you think of the play?"

"It was a lot of sentimental slosh," I said.

"You didn't like it?"

"No. But I enjoyed it nevertheless."

Marlon stared at me with a puzzled frown. "Sentimental slosh? You didn't like it? But you enjoyed it nevertheless? Now what in hell does that mean?"

"The performances were brilliant," I said. "Oscar Homolka

ABOVE: *Joan Tetzel, Frances Heflin, Marlon, Oscar Homolka, Mady Christians, and William Pringle.* (RICHARD TUCKER, GRAPHIC HOUSE)

BELOW: *Mady Christians, Marlon, Joan Tetzel, Frances Heflin, and Richard Bishop in* I Remember Mama. (RICHARD TUCKER, GRAPHIC HOUSE)

was marvelous, and so was Mady Christians. I enjoyed the acting, but I thought the play was dull. That's all."

"What about me?"

"What *about* you?" I said.

"Stop being so damn cute and tell me what you think about
my performance."

"Not bad," I said. "Considering."

"Considering? Considering *what*?"

"Considering it's your first professional job."

"It's not a showy part," he said. "There was nothing more
I could do with it."

That was true enough. He was playing the part of Nels,
the son who is fourteen years old in the first act and returns
in the latter part of the play as a youth of twenty. Marlon's
estimate was all that could be said about the part—a minor
role and bland.

With one important difference. When Marlon reappeared
as the grownup, handsome Nels, women in the audience gasped
in audible admiration. For the moment he would have to be
content with that visible sign of the future, for otherwise
Marlon's acting debut on the Broadway stage was decidedly
inauspicious.

He opened the door to his West End apartment without
using a key. There was a small crowd in the living room, and
I thought a party was in progress, but it turned out most of
the guests were my old acting chums from summer stock.
They let out yowls of delight when they recognized me, and
we all exchanged the effusive kisses and hugs of welcome,
making a grand show-biz display of affection.

Later, I learned these get-togethers at Marlon's place
occurred almost nightly. It was always open house, but only
for friends. Marlon was extremely wary of strangers. No new
faces were introduced into the crowd unless they were care-

fully screened. Consequently the regulars were extreme types —shy, sensitive, frightened people, or outlandishly uninhibited exhibitionists. A sensible, serious person who happened to wander in would soon discover he wasn't welcome.

Marlon left the room for a while. When he returned, he came to me and said, "Dodie is leaving tomorrow, and she wants to say good-bye to you."

"Where is she?" I said.

"In her bedroom. I'll take you to her."

I followed him to the end of a long hallway, and we stopped at a door that was half open.

"No need to knock," he said. "Go on in. She's expecting you."

Dodie was lying in bed, wearing a nightdress of light blue silk, her face shiningly cleansed of makeup and her ashblond hair brushed back behind her ears. She was reading a novel through Ben Franklin bifocals perched low on her nose. She looked up at me over the rim of the slim metal frame and said, "Please close the door and come over here and sit beside me." She slid to one side of the bed to make room for me, and I sat down.

"What are you reading?" I inquired.

"*Lady Chatterley's Lover*, by D. H. Lawrence," she told me.

It was a time when Lawrence's novel was considered a dirty book, legally obscene and available in the United States either in expurgated versions sold over the counter, or uncut if one knew a friendly dealer or had been to a Left Bank kiosk in Paris. The book Dodie was reading was not only unabridged, but as I examined it I saw that it was an autographed first edition as well.

"Is it all it's cracked up to be?" I asked her.

"It's quite good," she said, "but I prefer a good murder

mystery or a good psychological Western." She slipped off her reading glasses, closed the book, and put them aside. "Now, let's have a heart-to-heart talk, shall we?"

"All right," I said.

"Is your name really Frederick Stevens?"

"No," I said, "my real name is Carlo Fiore."

"Carlo Fiore," she repeated. "That's a beautiful name." I was grateful to her that she didn't follow up with the usual exclamation, "Why, oh, why did you change it?"

"Now that you're back," she went on, "what are your plans for the future?"

"I just learned that I'm eligible under the GI Bill to go to school, and I'm going to grab the opportunity."

"What will you study? Acting?"

"Yes. I want to continue with Piscator at the Dramatic Workshop. If I pass the intelligence test, that is. Talent aside, the VA wants to know if I'm intelligent enough to become an actor—that I'm not just an idiot dreamer."

"I'm sure you'll pass the test. You're not worried about it, are you?"

"No. A little nervous, perhaps, but not worried."

"How will you support yourself?"

"The VA pays for everything—tuition, textbooks, and so on. And they give you a subsistence besides."

"Will it be enough to live on?"

"Just about. But with a part-time job, I think I'll be able to manage."

"I was a little worried about you," Dodie said, "but I see now that I needn't have been. Forgive me for prying into your private affairs."

"Don't apologize," I said. "It's nice to know that you're concerned about me."

For a moment we lapsed into a silence that was neither awkward nor uncomfortable.

"Is there anything you want to ask me?" she inquired at last.

"Yes. May I ask what your plans are?"

"Of course. I'm going back home tomorrow morning."

"I know. Marlon told me. I'll miss you."

"And I'll miss you. And Bud. And New York."

"Then . . . why go?"

"Brando Senior called me long distance. He wants me home. And when he wants me, I come running. We've had some terrible quarrels and separated. Then reconciled, quarreled, and reconciled again. Said unforgivable things. It's a wonder we ever get together again. This has been one of our longest separations, and I'm glad he called. Just in time, too."

"Just in time?"

"Yes. I was beginning to fall off the wagon again. Hiding bottles all over the place, stealing a nip whenever I could. If he had delayed his call any longer I might have gone off on a two- or three-day bat. You and Bud sensed it, didn't you?"

"I . . . I really had no idea," I said, lying.

"Of course," she said. "You would have no way of knowing what was going on. But Bud would know. He knows the symptoms very well. I've put him through a lot of bad, bad times because of my drinking. God knows, I've tried to make it up to him."

"You *have* made it up to him," I tried to reassure her. "He couldn't have turned out better. He's the nicest, sweetest guy I know."

"Yes. He has turned out rather well, hasn't he?" The pride in her voice was obvious. "I hope he stays that way."

We both knocked wood to ward off bad luck.

"Well, I suppose you want to get back to your crowd," Dodie said. "If you ever need a friend, call me. Promise?"

"Promise," I told her.

"Well . . . good-bye for now."

I stood up to go, and she tilted her head back so that I could place a farewell kiss on her cheek.

As soon as I was back in the living room, Marlon approached me. I had the feeling he had been waiting for me.

"Is Dodie leaving tomorrow?" he asked anxiously. "Definitely leaving?"

"Yes," I said. "Were you expecting that she'd change her plans?"

"Yes. I was hoping she would."

"Why?"

"Because I asked her to," Marlon said. "I don't want her to go. I want her here. With me."

But next day she was gone.

CHAPTER FOUR

Aafter dodie left, Marlon had their large apartment to himself. There were three bedrooms and three baths, not including the maid's room and bath, a spacious living room, a dining room, a kitchen, and a den. It was a corner apartment on the eleventh floor, and every room had a panoramic view of the Hudson River and Riverside Park.

One foggy night the apartment was enveloped in a cloud, and a milky mist pressed against the closed windows. Marlon and I were sitting around talking, listening to music and sipping soft drinks. Deborah, the pretty girl who had been expelled with Marlon at Sayville, was with us. She was no longer a virgin.

After a time, Marlon grew bored and restless. He walked across the living room and opened a window. Like a ghostly serpent, the gray fog curled slowly into the room. Suddenly Marlon appeared to have gone mad. Assuming a dramatic pose, he cried out, "Good-bye, Freddie. Good-bye, Deborah." Then he quickly climbed over the windowsill and disappeared into the fog.

Deborah and I were momentarily stunned. We were sure that he hadn't jumped to his death, but it was nearly as terrifying to think that he was out there in the fog, clinging for his life by his fingertips eleven floors above a concrete sidewalk.

Deborah screamed after him, then pleaded, cajoled, and cursed him by turns, until she was completely hysterical. Marlon didn't respond. I managed to calm her down a little and succeeded in convincing her that in order to get Marlon to climb back into the room, we would have to stop playing his game. He was out there somewhere, listening, and enjoying our terror. To get him back in, we would have to keep quiet and ignore him. We went to the kitchen, sat down, and waited silently.

In a few minutes, Marlon sauntered in, calm as usual, and sat down at the table with us. Deborah was utterly shattered and couldn't hold back her tears or her anger. "You monster!" she screamed at him. "You fucking monster!" She dabbed at her mascaraed eyes with a handkerchief. "You've made me ruin my makeup."

Marlon apologized, but I could see that he was immensely pleased that we were so emotionally destroyed.

"That was a stupid stunt to pull," I said. "You might have killed yourself."

"I knew what I was doing," he said blandly. "I knew the rain pipe was there, and I held on to it."

"Those tin water drains are flimsy, and they're usually rotted with rust," I said. "It might have collapsed under your weight. How could you be sure it wouldn't?"

"That never occurred to me," he said.

Sometimes, especially on weekends, girls from Greenwich Village drifted uptown to join our get-togethers. They were exotic creatures, I thought, with long, wild hair and fantastic makeup, wearing peasant costumes, bare-legged, thonged leather sandals on their feet. They rarely joined in the general fun and gazed without self-consciousness at the proceedings. They never sat in chairs, but posed on cushions or on a rug and exuded a blatant, coarse sensuality. They were remote, lewd, and they waited for the crowd to thin.

They came, of course, to get laid, and laid they were. Occasionally I would wake up in the morning and find one of these predatory, sexually voracious creatures sleeping beside me, and then I would have to sort out my thoughts about the night before until I could remember how she got there. And not always succeeding.

One morning I woke up in the maid's room—it was the only unoccupied bed space in the apartment—and felt a gentle touch of fingertips on my stomach. I turned over and found myself staring directly at Marlon's broad back. His hand was groping tentatively, blindly, behind him. I watched as his hand moved down below my navel, crawling caterpillarlike along my abdomen to my pubic hair, until it came to rest at last on my penis.

Marlon sprang out of bed, as though he meant to hit the ceiling. He landed on the balls of his feet, actually bouncing once or twice.

"*Holy shit!*" he cried. "I thought I was in bed with a girl!"

[39]

"That's what I thought you thought," I said.

"Were you awake?"

"Yes," I said.

"Then why the hell didn't you stop me?"

"I wanted to see your reaction. You have fantastic reflexes. You'd win the gold medal in the Olympics for the high jump."

"Okay, you son of a bitch," Marlon said. "I'm going to get even with you for that. If it's the last thing I do, I'm going to get even."

A few days later, while we were sitting and talking in the apartment, I scratched my groin rather vigorously, and Marlon's face lit up with a wide, evil grin.

"You son of a bitch," he chortled. "I told you I'd get even with you, and I did. You've got the crabs."

(To those who have never seen a crab, let me describe one. A crab is a body louse that very much resembles in size and appearance this asterisk *, except that it is extremely active and prolific. It invades the pubic hair and is transferred from one person to another during sexual intercourse. Those who claim they caught the crabs because they had to sit on a public toilet seat in an emergency are usually lying.)

"I do not have the crabs," I said.

"Then why did you scratch your balls?"

"I had an itch."

"You had an itch because you have the crabs," Marlon insisted.

"I do not have the crabs," I repeated.

He slapped some money on the kitchen table and said, "I'll bet you five bucks you've got the crabs."

I covered his bet, lowered my pants and my undershorts, and we set about like monkeys, grooming and searching for crabs. After a long and careful examination of my pubic hair, Marlon finally had to admit that I had none. He was crest-fallen.

Pulling up my trousers and adjusting my clothing, I asked, "What made you so certain I had crabs?"

"Because that morning, after we went back to sleep, or rather after you did, I picked two crabs off me and put them on you."

"Pardon the pun," I said, "but that was a lousy trick."

I picked up the money, folded it neatly, and put it in my pocket.

Life at the apartment with Marlon and our friends was great fun, but I realized I had better get moving. I had pro-crastinated long enough, and I didn't want to get left behind. Some of my actor friends had been overwhelmed by the fierce competition for roles in Broadway plays. Many had faced up to their inadequacy, realized they were never going to make it, and had prudently gone back to where they came from— to get married, rear a family, or whatever. Some just dropped out of sight. I had done nothing but have a good time, and it couldn't last much longer.

It didn't. In due course the Veterans Administration notified me to report for my intelligence test. I examined the notification, not knowing whether to be happy or sorry. I was glad that something was happening to move me off center, but I was apprehensive because it seemed to me that I might prove abysmally ignorant. I needn't have worried. The test was so simple I could have passed with points to spare.

Several days later I got another letter from the VA. I was to report to the head of the psychiatric department, to a woman doctor. The letter provided no hint of whether I had passed or failed my examination. Its matter-of-fact prose was so spare that it began to sound rather ominous as I read it over.

When I arrived at the VA at the appointed time and gave my name to the receptionist, she pointed to one of several doors and told me to go right in. The doctor was expecting me.

The doctor was a meticulously groomed, buxom woman with smooth, pale skin and abundant brunette hair. She examined me through a pair of pince-nez glasses which pinched and wrinkled the bridge of her nose. Her spectacles were attached to a long black ribbon around her neck, which gave her a pleasant, rather old-world air. She offered me a seat and I sat down.

"Would you be willing to take another test?" she inquired.

"Did I fail the first?" I said.

"Oh, no," she replied. "Quite the opposite. You answered every question correctly."

"Then I can go to acting school?"

"Of course," she said. "You may apply at any school approved by the Veterans Administration. We give these tests only to determine one's aptitudes and to counsel one accordingly. But since you had a perfect score, we have no way to gauge your potential. This test won't be as simple as the other, but from it we will be able to determine your particular capability with greater accuracy. You don't have to take it if you don't want to, but since you have nothing to lose and something to gain—why not? Are you agreeable?"

"Yes," I said, "I'm agreeable."

"Good. We'll notify you after we've made arrangements for the time and place."

She stood up to indicate the interview was over, wished me good luck, and I left.

I was sent to a college in Brooklyn for my second examination. When I arrived, I was greeted by a pretty woman about twenty-four and was led immediately to an empty classroom. Seating me at the rear of the room, she placed a folio of twenty pages or more in front of me, walked up the aisle, sat at the teacher's desk, and opened a novel.

I shuffled quickly through the questionnaire and what I saw plunged me into despair. The academic level appeared to be far over my head. I skimmed through the pages, skipped the questions I thought were too difficult, and answered only the ones where I could put down anything with certainty.

As I reread the questions I had omitted, questions that seemed to be problems in chemistry, mathematics, or physics, it slowly dawned on me that the examination was actually a test for comprehensive reading ability. It was really nothing more than an exercise in deductive reasoning. I had found the key. The solution to each problem was contained within the question itself.

I sifted each question carefully, laboriously, until I had discovered the solution—so totally concentrated that when I looked up after completing the test, I was surprised to find that the bright afternoon had faded to dusk. Several hours had gone by, but it seemed to me no time at all.

In my final interview I was told that I possessed a superior intelligence and several aptitudes. I could become a lawyer, or an engineer, or an architect, or a teacher, or even a physicist, and with hard work I could graduate at the top of the class in college.

"College?" I said. "But I didn't graduate from high school. I quit after a year."

"We know that," the doctor said, leafing through my VA records. "We'll send you to high school and then to college, if you want to go."

"What about acting?" I asked her.

"You can always be an actor," she told me, smiling. "An education won't spoil you for the theater. It might even improve your chance for success. And then again, you must also consider the possibility of failing as an actor. Without an education, where will you be? What would you do for a living? If that turns out to be the case, you'll find a college degree very useful."

What she said made sense. I had seen a good many older, failed actors hanging around Broadway—in cafeterias, working at menial jobs in order to live, hustling for walk-ons or bits, waiting for The Part, which might never come.

"You don't have to make a decision now," she said. "Think it over. Take all the time you need. When you've decided what you want to do, call us."

"I've made my decision," I said.

"What is it?"

"I want to educate myself."

About this time Marlon had opened in *Truckline Cafe*, a new play by Maxwell Anderson. The critics had panned it, but they had high praise for Brando's performance. George Jean Nathan had written that "the acting company, except for Virginia Gilmore and Marlon Brando, was in major part second-rate. . . ." Later, in his *Theater Book of the Year*, Nathan had selected Marlon's portrayal in the play as one of the "especially interesting performances of the season."

Truckline Cafe had been playing for more than a week before I phoned Marlon to offer my belated congratulations.

"I'll leave a couple of tickets for you at the box office," he said.

"Great," I said. "What about Saturday?"

"What about *today*? The matinee."

[44]

"I can't. I've got classes."

"Classes?"

"Yeah, I'm going to the Borough Hall Academy in Flat-bush. It's a long story. I'll tell you all about it when I see you. Anyway, I can't make it today."

"But we're closing," Marlon said. "Don't you read the papers?"

I detected a note of derision in his voice. That was strange because Marlon himself never read newspapers, except for passing glances at headlines.

"Occasionally," I said. "Why?"

"Clurman and Kazan put an ad in the *Times* because they're pissed off at the critics for the bad reviews and forcing us to close."

"Will the ad help business, do you think?"

"Nope. So you'd better come as soon as you can."

"I can see tonight's performance. Then I won't have to miss school."

"Skip a few classes, can't you? Listen, I want to see you. A lot of shit has hit the fan since I saw you last, and I want to talk to you."

"What happened?"

"Dodie came back. She had another fight with Pop, and she left him. She's staying with me now. Or *was*. She's disappeared again."

"Where'd she go?"

"Who knows?"

"How long has she been missing?"

"Three days."

"Have you called the police?"

"No. Let's get off the phone and talk later. Can I expect you at the matinee?"

"Yes," I said.

"Good. I'll leave a couple of tickets for you."

"Just one. I'll be alone."

"I'll leave two. One for your hat and coat. We've got a lot of empty seats and we're papering the house. We're at the Belasco. Know where it is?"

"Yes," I said.

"Good. I'll see you after the show." He hung up.

That afternoon, fifteen minutes into the first act of *Truck-line Cafe*, I found myself agreeing with the critics. The main action of the play occurred offstage, so the actors had to describe the unseen episodes in long, explanatory dialogue. That doesn't make for exciting theater.

When I saw Marlon come on stage, I was shocked. I hadn't seen him for several weeks, and he had lost so much weight that he looked emaciated. Of course his debilitated appearance did enhance the characterization of the mentally embattled soldier he was portraying. But endangering one's health to give verisimilitude to a performance was carrying an actor's responsibility to his role too far.

What surprised me even more was Marlon's lack of acting technique, or, rather, his total disregard of the stagecraft he had learned. He broke every rule in the book. His posture was a sloppy slouch, his head was almost always bowed, and he kept his hands rammed in his back pockets. Often he turned away from the audience and delivered his lines upstage, throwing away many of his speeches in shapeless sounds. Marlon always spoke in a modulated voice, and his speech and diction, especially on the stage, had always been clear and precise. But this was the first time I had heard him mumble. Several people in the audience whispered loudly, "What did he say?" "I can't hear him." "Why doesn't he take the marbles out of his mouth?"

The young wife in the play, portrayed by Ann Shepherd,

gripped Sage's arm (Sage McRae was the name of the character Marlon played) and beseeched him to tell her what was troubling him. She reminded him that she was his wife who loved him and that she had a right to know what had happened to him in the Army. Sage looked at his wife as if she weren't there, said nothing, then turned away from her again. It was a moving interpretation of a soul in anguish—inarticulate, withdrawn, almost catatonic.

This is strong stuff in the theater, and every actor knows it is suicide in a performance to bring your audience to a high pitch and then deny them the release of a fitting climax. If an actor fails to achieve this climax for the audience, his whole performance goes down the drain.

The play was slowly dying on its feet, and the audience was becoming restless, when at this low point, during which many of the spectators were debating whether to leave, the plot abruptly introduced a jolting turn. The audience was tossed the startling revelation that Sage, the psychologically shattered soldier, had murdered his wife and was hiding somewhere in the vicinity. A posse had been formed to hunt him down, and the populace was warned to take precautions for their safety. The fugitive was armed and dangerously deranged.

The cafe was deserted at closing time, and the waitress, preparing to lock up, was turning off the lights. Sage, drenched to the skin and shaking with a teeth-chattering chill, entered the darkened scene quietly. The waitress gasped with fright when she saw the fugitive killer. In a weak, plaintive voice, Sage assured her that he would do her no harm. He only wanted a moment's rest, a cup of hot coffee, before he gave himself up to the police. The waitress, seeing that he was near collapse, was filled with compassion. She poured a cup of coffee for him and placed it at a small table at center stage.

Sage sat down and, for a little warmth, huddled himself over the steaming coffee. Then he quickly drained the cup, and the waitress refilled it. This show of humanity moved Sage to confess the circumstances that had led him to the murder of his wife.

While fighting overseas, he told the waitress, he had met a recruit newly arrived from the United States and they quickly became buddies. The recruit was heartbroken because he had recently met a girl in the States, and just when they had fallen in love with each other he had been shipped overseas. As the recruit described the intimate details of his tender love affair, Sage, to his horror, became aware that his new comrade was actually talking to him about his wife. The recruit had unwittingly revealed a wife's infidelity to her own husband. Sage took the news of his wife's unfaithfulness in stunned silence. His wife had written regularly, and each letter had proclaimed her undying love for him. The tone of her letters had been so sincere that he believed her absolutely. To realize now that his wife's letters were nothing more than a packet of lies threw him into shock, and he had been hospitalized. The doctors diagnosed his condition as battle fatigue, and he was sent home on furlough to recover.

His wife appeared genuinely glad to see him home again, and it seemed to Sage that she was still very much in love with him. But because his trust in her was destroyed, he could not believe her protestations of love for him, and since life without love or faith seemed no longer worth living, he decided to kill her and himself.

As Marlon, playing Sage, unfolded this story in a long monologue to the waitress, he created the scene so vividly that I could have sworn I heard the gun shots reverberate in the theater when he came to the climax. With his wife dead,

Sage told the waitress, he placed the gun at his temple, hesitated, and found he lacked the courage to pull the trigger. He decided to kill himself another way. He would swim out in the lake as far as he could, until he was totally exhausted and had to drown. But in the middle of the vast, frigid lake, he had lost his courage again, turned back, and by some miracle found the strength to swim to shore and make his way to the cafe.

At this point in the play, the posse was heard approaching, and the waitress offered to hide him. But Sage made no attempt to escape. Several burly men stormed into the cafe, handguns drawn, pulled Sage to his feet, handcuffed him, and, as they dragged him away, threatened him with lynching. But the threat of death held no terror now for Sage. He went out with the posse willingly, almost dancing, eager for his annihilation.

With that exit, the audience rose to its feet as one person and stopped the show to give Marlon a standing ovation. That inspired performance, to this day, remains for me one of the most thrilling experiences I have ever had in the theater.

After the matinee, we went to Marlon's apartment on West End Avenue for a light supper. He was quiet and hardly touched his food. I thought he looked terrible. His eyes were dark hollows and his complexion was ashen. I wondered if he was using stimulating drugs to heighten the energy level of his performance.

"You look terrible," I said. "You're not taking drugs, are you?"

"Of course not," he answered. "I don't want to talk about myself. Let's talk about you. What's all this about classes?"

"The VA gave me an intelligence test and discovered that I'm a potential genius. So they're subsidizing my education."

"Are you giving up acting to become a genius?"

"I haven't made up my mind about that yet," I said. "I might."

Marlon shook his head sadly. "I'd rather you'd stay as you are—a sweet, untutored wop."

"Fuck you," I said.

The door was flung open, and Dodie appeared. A black cabbie, burdened with parcels, followed her into the living room and placed the load of packages on a sofa.

"Thank you," Dodie said, handing the cabbie a bill.

He gave the bill a swift glance, thanked her for the generous tip, and left.

Dodie took off her camel's-hair coat, wide-brimmed felt hat, and overshoes, and began to unwrap the packages. She looked marvelous, as though she had spent a restful week in the country.

Anger and relief struggled on Marlon's face. He was angry because her disappearance had caused him a great deal of worry, but at the same time he was happy to see her home again, safe, sound, and sober.

We behaved as though Dodie hadn't vanished for several days. We pretended that she had just returned from an afternoon of shopping on Fifth Avenue. We lounged, sipped coffee, and talked of inconsequential things until it was time for Marlon to leave for his evening performance.

Marlon turned to me. "Think you can bear to see the play again?" he asked. "You can watch it from the wings if you like."

"I think I might manage it," I said, rising from my chair.

In fact, I was eager to see how Marlon prepared himself for that big scene. Most actors who have to start a scene at the top of their emotions rarely make an entrance cold. They usually execute certain offstage exercises to pump up their

[51]

PPOSITE: *Marlon as he appeared at the time he was laying in* Truckline Cafe. (FRIEDMAN-ABELES)

creative juices. I supposed that Marlon would have to draw on a plentiful supply of adrenalin to meet the requirements of his role. I was more than a little curious to see how he would accomplish it.

To stand in the wings during a performance is an extraordinary experience. You are assailed simultaneously by three different and distinct atmospheres. One is the backstage atmosphere itself, where the actors nervously wait for their cue to enter. Then there is the atmosphere onstage, listening to the actors performing. Finally, there is the atmosphere in the theater, where the audience vibrations flow toward the stage—or retreat from it, depending on the quality of the play and its performance.

Several minutes before Marlon made his entrance for the final scene, I saw two stagehands station themselves at the bottom of a wrought-iron spiral stairway, holding buckets of water at the ready. Marlon appeared, placed himself at the foot of the stairs, braced himself as the stagehands splashed him from head to foot, then he leaped up the stairway, taking two or three steps at a time. He ran up and down the stairs at a furious pace, as though he was trying to outdistance some pursuing disaster, timing the instant of his entrance to the split second.

When he appeared onstage, half drowned, shivering, and staggering with fatigue, the vibrations of the audience suddenly surged toward the stage in a huge, single wave. From the moment of his entrance, Marlon held the audience transfixed, just as he had done during the matinee performance. After his exit he was given once more, a tumultuous standing ovation.

From my post backstage I watched Marlon with amazement. I saw that his gradual metamorphosis from dilettante to dedicated actor was complete. It had been a short road from Sayville.

"Jesus!" I said to him later. "No wonder you look so wasted! You're lucky the play is closing. A long run would kill you."

Certainly it was a high point in his career. I remember, years later, when he had been in a succession of flop pictures, we were talking on the phone one day, and unconsciously I began talking about his past successes as though he were dead.

"Thanks for putting me in the past tense," he said sarcastically. "All that talk about 'used to be.' "

"I was thinking about *Truckline*," I said.

"I was insane then."

"You could use some of that insanity now," I said.

CHAPTER FIVE

BRANDO SENIOR arrived in
New York, ostensibly to see his son perform in a revival of
George Bernard Shaw's *Candida*, starring Katharine Cornell
and Cedric Hardwicke. The play was scheduled to open on
April 3, 1946, which coincidentally happened to be twenty-two
years from the time Marlon was born in Omaha, Nebraska. I
suspected there was another reason for Marlon's father to be in
town. Dodie was still there, and I was sure he wanted to try
to reconcile with her once more and take her back with him to
Libertyville, Illinois, where they were then living.

He couldn't have come at a better time as far as the
weather was concerned. Spring had been late, but after a win-

ter of unbroken, filthy days, the sun had come through the low-hanging clouds to give us some perfect days. One warm, bright morning I had a touch of spring fever and decided to skip a day of school. I called Marlon to invite him for a walk in Riverside Park.

"I'd like that," Marlon said, "but my family is here and I'd better hang around. Why don't you come up and join us?"

"Is your father there?"

"Yes, and I want you to meet him."

I hesitated. "Okay. I'll be there in about ten minutes."

"Later," Marlon said, hanging up.

I had met all of the Brandos except Marlon's father and had been as instantly friendly with them as I had been with Marlon, but I had a strong premonition that Senior and I were not going to get on. But sooner or later it was inevitable that we were going to meet, and I concluded that now was as good a time as any.

I pressed the bell. The door opened presently, and Marlon, neatly dressed in shirt and tie and looking rather subdued, appeared.

"Hi, Freddie," he said, smiling wanly. "Come on in."

I followed him through the foyer to the living room and found myself standing before Senior, who rose from his seat. We were introduced and shook hands.

It was reasonable to expect that father and son would resemble each other to some degree, and I was prepared for that, but Marlon's resemblance to his father was remarkable. They were the same height, and both had the same bull neck and bullet-shaped head, the same broad, sloping shoulders, gladiator chest, and powerfully muscled arms. Senior was heavier and thicker, but looking at him was like seeing a physical projection of what Marlon would be in his middle years.

In a tweedy, country-squire kind of way, Senior was on the

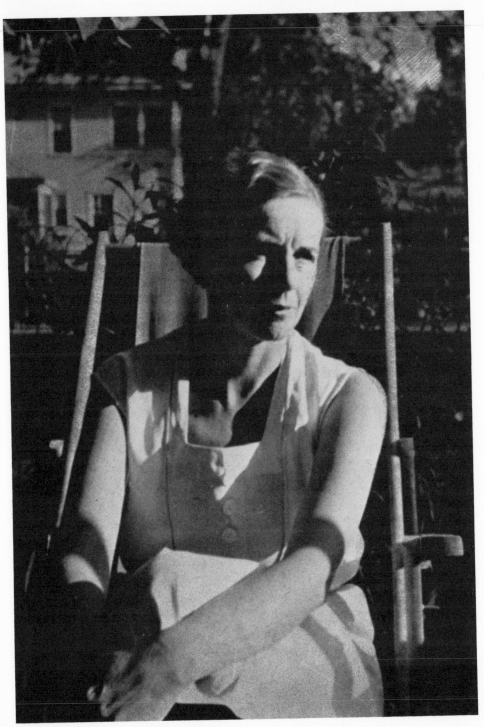

Dorothy Pennebaker Brando, "Dodie."

dapper side, and evidently he had already found an excellent barber. His sandy hair, which was growing thin at the top, was trimmed just so, his bristly mustache was close-cropped, his fingernails were precisely shaped and brightly buffed, and his cordovan shoes shone richly. His stiff military bearing put me in mind of a cavalryman on dress parade, mounted on a well-trained, well-groomed horse.

We sat and regarded each other and made small talk. A death-in-the-family atmosphere prevailed in the room. Never had I seen the apartment so tidy and clean. Even the ash-trays gleamed like crystal. Everyone sat composed, and the conversation was restricted to the barest essentials.

"Would you like a cup of coffee?"

"Yes, thank you."

"Sugar?"

"One, please."

"Cream?"

"Just a touch."

I got the feeling that some distant kin had been laid out in a coffin in the adjoining room. During the prolonged silences in the conversation there was a restless crossing and recrossing of legs.

Once, when Dodie crossed hers, her skirt hiked up above her knees. She pulled her dress down to cover them, and from above, in Dodie's perspective, her legs appeared to be properly covered. Sitting across from her, however, we saw that her skirt was caught up beneath her and that the undersides of her legs were exposed. It was not all that revealing, nor shocking in any way, so no one said anything. To call her attention to it would only have caused her needless embarrassment.

I could see Senior's growing agitation, and he kept shifting his weight about in his chair until he finally snapped, "Dodie! Adjust your dress!"

Her eyes examined the full length of her frock, found nothing to adjust, and she looked up, perplexed.

"Your skirt is snagged under you," Senior told her.

"Oh!" Dodie exclaimed. She lifted herself a few inches above her chair, ran her hand under her to smooth her skirt, and settled down again. She smiled to disguise her embarrassment, but her eyelids twitched with an uncontrollable tic.

Jocelyn, Marlon's sister, tried to carry the conversation in her usual vivacious way, like the actress she was. She was two or three years older than her brother and liked to tell stories, acting out all the parts, which vastly entertained her friends. Now I could see that it was frustrating for her to keep her natural exuberance in check, although she did her best to do that and be entertaining at the same time. Jocelyn was a pocket-size edition of her mother, and she had inherited Dodie's distinctive walk and style.

Frances Brando, next youngest in the family, was about twenty-three. She was an art student, so short her feet barely reached the floor when she sat down, but possessed of a plump, voluptuously rounded figure. Except for a touch of rouge on her lips, she wore no makeup, and she dressed in plain, rustic clothes. Frances hated big cities. She preferred the vast, open plains and the brisk, clean air of the Midwest. In the family group now, she sat in her chair with her hands folded in her lap, looking out of place. It was obvious that she yearned to return to her family ranch in Libertyville, Illinois, just as soon as possible.

After my arrival, Senior had not looked at me once. As far as he was concerned, it appeared, the chair I occupied was empty. His evident disapproval of me bordered on rudeness, and I was depressed.

Marlon saw that I was ill at ease, and he came to my rescue.

"No school today?" he inquired.

"I'm playing hooky," I said. "It's a rare day for New York, and I had to get outdoors."

"Let's go then," Marlon said. "Let's go for that walk you wanted. And let's take Dutchie."

"All right," I said, almost springing to my feet.

Dutchie was the family's Great Dane, an aging, dignified Harlequin going gray around the eyes and ears. She had been drowsing in a corner of the room, but when she saw Marlon go for her leash, she scampered to him and thrust her head eagerly into the leather collar.

I shook hands with Senior and said that I was glad to have met him and that I looked forward to seeing him again soon. He pumped my hand once, or maybe twice, said nothing in reply, and sat down again. I waved good-bye to everyone, and Marlon, Dutchie, and I went out the door.

Outside in the street, I couldn't help taking a deep breath that was plainly a sigh of relief. As we walked toward the park, Marlon said, "Well, what do you think of my father?"

I suppressed a nearly irresistible impulse to say that I thought him a snob, a bully, and a bore. But one doesn't say such things about a friend's father in any case, and although I knew that Marlon and Senior were no great admirers of each other, just the same it *was* his father and no one likes to hear his father denigrated, even if he does it himself.

"I wouldn't kick off my shoes, stretch out my legs, and pick my nose in his company," I said carefully. "I'm afraid he didn't like me. Not a bit."

"My father's insecure," Marlon said. "He's a frightened man."

"Oh, come on!" I said. "Your father frightened? Of me?"

"Not of *you* in particular, you conceited, hypersensitive Sicilian! You happened to meet him at the wrong time. Right after you called we all had a talk to try to straighten out certain situations that are bent out of shape. Pop's afraid he's losing his grip on the family, so he laid down some ultimatums. I *hate* ultimatums! And pretty soon we were in the middle of shout-down, then—you came in."

"No wonder." That was all I could think of to say.

Dutchie started tugging at the leash, jerking Marlon a few paces ahead of me. I quickened my step to keep up with them. I noticed a number of fire hydrants and some fine-looking trees equidistantly spaced at the edge of the curb.

"Why doesn't Dutchie stop at trees or fire hydrants, like other dogs?" I asked.

"Dutchie has a favorite spot in the park. She won't go anyplace else unless she has to. But locked in the house alone, she'd shit in your hat and piss on your shoes, just to remind you of your negligence."

A Pekingese had slipped its leash and ran yapping and snapping at Dutchie. In her great urgency, the big dog knocked over the noisy little creature without even breaking her stride. The tiny animal's mistress, a small, elderly lady, hurried over, scooped up her darling, and shouted an obscenity after us that was so rank it could have pinned a wrestling Turk to the mat.

We entered the park. The habitués were out in force to sit on benches in the warmth of the sun. Some read newspapers, magazines, or books, while others, with eyes closed, held their faces up to catch the direct rays to get a tan.

Dutchie's favorite spot turned out to be in the center of a broad lawn, encircled by a foot-high, wrought-iron border. Tender shoots of newly planted grass sparsely covered the dark earth, still moist from the melted snow. Beside herself with joy, Dutchie spun around in a circle, her nose sniffing the ground. Finally she settled on a spot, squatted, faced the crowd, which by now was watching her with frozen apprehension, and with her ears and head held high in sheer rapture, she squeezed out turd upon turd upon turd, forming a nearly perfect pyramid.

Magazines, newspapers, books, and everything else were lowered at once, disclosing the flabbergasted, disgusted glares of the park habitués. We tried to pull Dutchie away, but she wouldn't budge. The spectators clacked their tongues, shook their heads, and murmured, "Shame! Shame!"

"Can't you read the sign?" one of them shouted. "Read the sign!"

Marlon and I turned to see a freshly painted shingle that read:

LET THEM NOT SAY

UNTO YOUR SHAME

THAT ALL WAS BEAUTY HERE

BEFORE YOU CAME

I looked at Marlon, but he had resumed watching Dutchie. He seemed to be enjoying the occasion as much as she was and was equally oblivious of the onlookers' disapproval. But he was thinking about something else because he turned to me and said, "What the hell have you been doing to yourself? You look like Dutchie's pile of shit."

Then I had to make the worst admission of my life. I told him that the night before I had met a girl I'll call Vicki. She was a high-priced hooker and a junk joy-popper (someone who occasionally shoots up with heroin). We had gone to bed together, and she had talked me into shooting up with her. It wouldn't take long before I was hooked—on Vicki and on heroin. But I told Marlon, "Don't worry. I won't get hooked.

I know what I'm doing," which I had deluded myself into believing.

As we walked back to the apartment, Marlon seemed saddened. Then he said, "Freddie, I think it's the biggest mistake you can make. The first fix is the worst one."

Two days later Marlon opened in *Candida*. It was for him a tremendous leap from Maxwell Anderson's contemporary, naturalistic *Truckline Cafe* to Shaw's highly stylized play, and I wondered if his talent was versatile enough to bridge it. There was another pitfall confronting him too. Burgess Meredith had played Marchbanks in a previous production and done it so beautifully it had made him a star. Inevitably, Marlon would be compared with Meredith, and if his performance fell below the standard of his predecessor, he would no doubt consider himself a failure.

In the end, the critics were split. Some said Marlon's performance was excellent, while others nailed him to the wall. I was especially sorry to read Nathan's review. Here, in part, is what he wrote in his *Year Book of 1945-46*:

> . . . In the all-important role of Marchbanks, so ably handled in the earlier revival by Burgess Meredith, Marlon Brando's young poet's weakness becomes almost wholly a matter of weak acting. That Brando, who is a comparative novice, is not without potentialities is likely. But, with astute directors advising him, he will in time learn that consistency in character delineation does not necessarily call for a consistently monotonous manner of speech, that sensitiveness lies in more than a pale makeup and an occasionally quivering hand, and that a picture of physical weakness is better to be limned than by acting like a puppy ever in fear of a cat, as one of moral courage is better to be suggested than by staccato expectorations of one's opinions.

What I think Nathan meant was that Marchbanks was beyond Marlon's experience and comprehension, that the role was too simply conceived and superficially played.

Well . . . maybe. In any case, having read Nathan's review, I intended to see for myself. I had a couple of tickets for a matinee, and I was taking Elaine Stritch with me.

Our seats were in the third row center. I was closer to the actors than I liked to be. You could see the lines painted on their faces, perspiration beading their brows, notice a button hanging loose on a sleeve, or see a small tear in the hem of a skirt. Trifles, I know, but such trifles are apt to distract a viewer and inhibit his suspension of disbelief.

The Cort Theater was packed and noisy, but the audience hushed quickly when the house lights went down and the curtain rose.

The first act ticked away as accurately as a Swiss watch and was about as entertaining as the second hand sweeping over its face. The actors never missed a point. Every syllable was enunciated clearly. The timing was perfect, not a beat missed. What did it matter that the comedy was "antiquated buffoonery," as someone had called it? Did it matter that Cedric Hardwicke played his part as broadly as a circus clown? Or that Wesley Addy was as lifelike as a ventriloquist's dummy? Or that Katharine Cornell's Candida was a flawlessly painted mannikin? Only Mildred Natwick's Proserpine had some life, or at least some resemblance to it. I was hoping for a small accident, some jarring note, like a doorknob coming off in an actor's hand, or a chair collapsing under him. Something, anything, to break the monotony!

I got my wish when Marlon appeared on stage. His presence snapped the mainspring of that clockworks. Until then, all the entrances and exits had been made exactly on cue, but when Marlon entered, he came in way, way off the beat. He seemed horrified to find himself onstage. Under his makeup he was deadly white. When he crossed to the sofa, he sat with his feet tucked under him, and his hand shook as he ran his fingers along the bridge of his nose. Stage fright had stricken him dumb, I thought. He didn't speak for so long that the actors exchanged nervous glances. The only sound to be heard was the prompter's voice whispering in the wings—whispering at first, then almost shouting the lines. Still Marlon remained silent.

Elaine and I slid down in our seats, held hands and squeezed hard in agony. Was Marlon only acting fear? Was he doing it deliberately? For effect? Or was he really too scared to speak? The audience sat up on the edge of their seats. Expectation was in the air.

Marlon drew in the reins on his scattered concentration, gained more and more confidence, and gradually, almost inch by inch, he slipped into the skin of the character he was portraying. As the play progressed, the portrait of Marchbanks emerged. Marlon was etching the oddball poet to the life.

Some actors, when they cannot make contact with another actor or actress, will "substitute" the other—in their mind's eye—with someone they know in real life with whom they have shared an emotional experience. It is a legitimate device, which Marlon has used often and effectively in his career. In the third act, when Marchbanks declared his love for Candida and pleaded with her to come away with him, although he could offer her nothing but despair and suffering, I would take an oath that Marlon had metamorphosed Katharine Cornell into Dodie. If he had, in fact, used that actor's conjuring device, he succeeded admirably.

At the end of the play, when the curtain came down and the actors stepped forward one by one, Marlon was given the loudest, most enthusiastic applause—the "comparative novice," against those experienced, distinguished actors who formed the cast.

An actor needs no critic to tell him whether he was good or not.

CHAPTER SIX

Buzzing about the new actor called Brando, the matinee audience left the theater slowly, reluctantly, as though trying to prolong, if only for a few seconds, an exciting experience.

Elaine Stritch and I hurried through the crowd to see Marlon in his dressing room. At closer range, I could see that his makeup and costume were perfectly in character with the role of Marchbanks. His clothes hung loosely on him and created the illusion that he was extremely thin, with a caved-in chest, and he wore his hair long, in soft, large waves, making an appropriate frame for his pale poet's face.

"Your getup is perfect," I said. "Who did it?"

"That's a silly-ass question," Marlon said. "*I* did. With a little help from the playwright's description, of course."

I should have known better than to ask. Marlon always creates his own getup; he believes that it's an important part of his interpretation of a character. Makeup artists and costume designers are craftsmen who paint and dress the actor according to the instructions he gives them. Actors who depend totally on the imagination of others to paint and dress them are usually second-rate.

Elaine asked Marlon if he had been as stricken with stage fright as he appeared when he made his entrance.

"I sure was," he said, grinning. "It's a good thing the character was supposed to enter scared shitless. I used my stage fright and incorporated it in the part."

Marlon always enjoyed embarrassing Elaine, so as he talked he casually dropped his pants as the first article to be removed in the ritual of undressing. She stifled a cry and clapped her hands over her eyes. Marlon was wearing jockey shorts, but Elaine was certain he was balls-naked from the waist down. With her eyes covered, she dashed to the door, murmuring something about an appointment with a hairdresser, and slammed out.

"She's twenty-two," Marlon said as soon as she was gone, "and do you know—she's still a virgin."

"Who? Elaine?" I said.

"No. Edna May Oliver," Marlon replied. "Of course I mean Elaine. Who else was here?"

"Well, she's lived a strict and sheltered life," I said lamely.

"I'll say. She's Catholic. Her uncle, or some close relative, is a bigwig in the Church. A bishop or a cardinal or something. Poor girl."

There was a knock at the door and Marlon quickly pulled on a pair of slacks as he shouted permission to come in.

[67]

Two girls entered—bright, chic and sexy. Speaking with New England accents, they introduced themselves, congratulated Marlon on his performance, and sat down in the chairs he offered them. They sat with legs crossed, lit cigarettes, and gazed at us with clear, untroubled eyes. For a long moment, while no one spoke, they examined Marlon from head to foot, sizing him up. Then they turned to me and took my measure in the same way. Apparently they were satisfied with what they saw because they invited us to stay overnight with them on a friend's yacht, moored in the Hudson River. They were obviously horny and looking for some fancy action. I signaled Marlon to accept the invitation, but to my utter disbelief he turned them down. They shrugged their shoulders, expressed regrets, and got up and left, as cool as when they came in.

"Why the hell did you say no?" I exploded. "You've turned down two of the classiest bitches I've ever seen. Just looking at them gave me a hard-on."

"Save it for tonight," Marlon said, "because I've got us a date with two chicks with asses like hearts in a valentine."

I was still dubious, and even more so when our dates turned out to be two waitresses in a small Greek restaurant on the seamy side of town. They weren't at all pretty. In fact, they had nothing to recommend them but their youth. Both were brunettes, heavy at the hip, and hairy. They had thick, unplucked eyebrows, faint mustaches, and looked as though they could use a bath.

"Are you out of your fucking mind?" I said to Marlon when I had the chance. "From what standpoint—*what* makes you prefer these broads to those lovely creatures we saw this afternoon?"

"My dick," Marlon said, arching his eyebrows. "Where my dick goes, *I* go."

At that, the night didn't turn out badly. The Greek waitresses were modest and charming—a bit too musky, perhaps, but eager to please, passionate, and indefatigable. They had put aside a bottle of absinthe—not Pernod, but genuine absinthe, the green, wormwood liquor that drove Oscar Wilde and Toulouse-Lautrec insane—and we all had several glasses of that powerful illegal brew.

Several days later, Marlon held his hands up to my face, palms thrust forward, wiggled his fingers, and said, "I've got those things again."

"Crabs?"

Marlon nodded.

"Not again," I said.

"Yep. Crabs. Again," he admitted disconsolately.

But the crabs did not prevent him from concluding a successful run in *Candida*, and after it closed he pursued what appeared to be a passion for playing poets that year by taking on another such character, Stanislas, a young revolutionary, in Jean Cocteau's *The Eagle Has Two Heads*, starring Tallulah Bankhead.

The play went out of town for a tryout. Within a few days, Marlon was out of the play and back in town. He told me that Tallulah had tried to seduce him and that he just couldn't make it.

She had asked him, he said, to come to her hotel suite one night to discuss certain changes in the script. When he arrived, she greeted him at the door as though they were both playing one of the oldest scenes in the business. She was wearing a slinky, silk dressing gown so sheer it outlined the nipples of her breasts and clearly defined the Mound of Venus. "She had a small bouquet of purple flowers pinned at her hip," Marlon went on, "and she was as drunk as a skunk." Looking past her, he saw a dimly lit room and heard romantic music playing softly.

Marlon entered, quite ill at ease. He was ready to admit that Tallulah was a beautiful woman, but she was simply not his cup of tea. Moreover, when she spoke to him in that husky voice of hers, her breath almost bowled him over. "Man, was her breath foul!" he told me, reminiscently. "It came out of her mouth and hung in the air like a poisonous mist." But the more he tried to escape her advances, the more aggressive and talkative she became.

"I just couldn't stand it any longer," Marlon confessed, "and out of desperation, I copped the plea that I was a virgin. Of course she didn't believe me, but she was so flabbergasted that she turned me out of her place, *tout suite.*"

Next day, Tallulah asked him to come to her dressing room. When he knocked, the door was opened so quickly that it gave him a start.

"Young man," Tallulah shouted, obviously in a rage, "if you're a Communist, you're in for a rude awakening." And she slammed the door in his face.

In spite of this obscure threat, the play went on. In one scene, Marlon as Stanislas was required to climb a flight of stairs, then to break into tears and turn so that the audience would be able to see that he was crying. The tears had to be on tap instantly, an almost impossible trick. Marlon was not daunted, however, and came up with a solution. He placed a dab of Vick's Vaporub on the underside of the handrailing and, as he climbed the stairs, he smeared his fingertips with the stuff and rubbed it in the corners of his eyes so that when he turned it would appear to the audience that his cheeks were glistening with tears.

Tallulah was puzzled by the strong scent of menthol in the air and wondered if someone had a cold. And if someone *did* have a cold, she reasoned, in her forthright way, that *someone* should stay at home in bed instead of spreading germs all

Tallulah Bankhead and Marlon in The Eagle Has Two Heads.
(RICHARD TUCKER, GRAPHIC HOUSE)

over the goddamn place. It didn't help when Marlon explained what he had been doing to fake the tears. Tallulah exploded, and soon after Marlon and the cast parted company.

He was replaced by Helmut Dantine. A wag of a critic in one tryout city remarked that the actors looked as though they had been recruited at the local lumberyard. When the play finally opened at the Plymouth Theater in New York, it was soundly trounced by the critics and closed after twenty-nine performances.

While Marlon was jousting with Tallulah, I began thinking of Vicki again and I couldn't get her out of my mind, even though I certainly didn't want to turn on junk, nor did I want to get caught up in that devouring sex of hers. I resisted the temptation to call, but I knew I was kidding myself. I just had to see her again.

When I called, she asked me to come right over. She was in her bathrobe when she greeted me. Before we even spoke, we kissed, and we could hardly wait to undress and hop in bed. It was only after we had had several orgasms that we calmed down enough to talk.

"Where have you been?" she asked. "Why haven't you called?"

I hesitated, then decided to tell the truth. "I don't want to get emotionally involved with anyone. I don't want to fall in love with you."

"Why not?"

"You'd be bad for me."

"How do you mean—bad?"

"We'd never get out of bed. We'd fuck our lives away."

"I can think of worse ways of throwing away a life."

"But I've got other things to do. I want to make something of myself."

"I can help you," Vicki said eagerly.

"How?"

"I can help support you. Help put you through school. And I'll take care of you," she added—and kissed me.

We stayed in bed for more than two days, making love, smoking marijuana, listening to music, letting the phone ring unanswered, ordering food from the corner delicatessen, inventing ways of making love, exploring each other until we didn't know which way to turn.

A few days later I went for a walk in Central Park with Marlon. He had been offered a role in Noël Coward's *Present Laughter* but had sent Noël a scathing letter of refusal, talking rather loftily about not having anything to do with frivo-

*Marlon, Steve Hill, Jonathan Harris, and Harold Gray
in* A Flag is Born. (GRAPHIC HOUSE, INC.)

lous comedies in such troubled times. It was an expensive
gesture. He was turning down the highest salary anyone had
offered him to date, about five hundred dollars a week. Instead,
he chose to work for fifty dollars a week to play the Jewish
refugee, David, in *A Flag Is Born*, a play produced by the

[73]

American League for a Free Palestine. The profits were used to transport displaced Jews to their Holy Land. Marlon was rehearsing in this play on the beautiful, late-summer evening when we walked in the park, savoring the approaching autumn in the brisk air.

"How's school?" Marlon asked.

"It's a fucking bore," I said.

"Then why don't you quit?"

"And do what?"

"And do what you really want to do."

"I don't know what I really want to do."

"Don't you want to be an actor?"

"I don't know."

"A writer?"

"I don't know."

"But you must want to do *something*," Marlon said. "Be something. You can't be a playboy all your life."

We walked on for a little while, both thinking, trying to plumb each other's thoughts without talking. Then, suddenly, Marlon was shaking with laughter.

"What's so funny?" I said.

"*You* are," Marlon said. "*I* am. *People* are. This whole fucking life is funny. And I'm not going to take it seriously. Not yet." Then, with one of his swift changes: "I'll bet I can jump higher than you."

"I know you can. And so do you. But how many damn times do you have to prove it?" I said.

"Here. Let's see who can touch the second branch of this tree," he said and promptly leaped up and tapped it with ease.

I made a halfhearted jump and didn't get within a foot of it.

"Come on," Marlon said. "You can do better than that. You're not even trying. Try this time. Really try."

I jumped up again, missed by two or three inches, and wanted to give it up.

"No, no," Marlon said. "I'll bet you'll tap it on the next try."

I leaped again and missed. Jumped again and again and kept missing by a hair. Why in hell am I jumping up and down like this, like an idiot? I thought. I've got things to do, problems to unravel. And here I am bouncing up and down like a crazy pogo stick without a care in the world. I put all I had into one final leap and barely scratched the branch with my fingernails.

Marlon was delighted. "There! You see? You did it. That's one of your problems, Freddie. You give up too easily. Come on, let's go to the Professor's for spaghetti."

The spaghetti at the Professor's had unique qualities, and so did the meatballs. A dish of spaghetti cost twenty-five cents, and the meat balls were a dime each. If you ate the spaghetti and meatballs while they were steaming hot, they were delicious. If you waited any length of time—say, the time it took to go to the john, urinate, and wash your hands—you would return to find that the spaghetti had congealed into a solid mass. You could spear it with your fork and hold it up in the air and it wouldn't unravel or drop. It would remain a firm, hard lump, like a piece of present-day pop-art sculpture. Knowing that, whenever the waiter insinuated the spaghetti around our elbows in front of us, we dove into it with our forks before the dishes hit the table.

It was toward this unlikely pasta emporium, then, that we made our way from the park. The restaurant was some-where around Forty-eighth Street and Eighth Avenue. As we walked, I remarked, "It must be great fun working with Paul Muni. He's a fine actor."

"That he is," Marlon agreed.

[75]

"What's he like?" I said.

"He's a funny old coot from the Yiddish Theater—you know, theatrical as all get out. And he likes to be pampered. His wife wraps his shoulders in a shawl and she keeps adjusting it constantly when it slips, as though he were an invalid."

"There's nothing of the invalid about him on stage. He's a powerful actor."

"He's that too," Marlon agreed again. "And he's also an absolute egomaniac. Once Luther [Luther Adler, the director] put his hand on Muni's shoulder to get his attention. Muni turned around and slapped Luther's hand for touching him. He kept slapping at his hand until Luther backed away out of reach. Luther hasn't dared touch him since."

"How do you get along with Muni?" I asked.

Marlon sighed. "Oh, I dunno. All right. I guess."

"What's the matter?"

"Well, I don't think Muni's convinced that I'm serious about acting. He thinks I'm some kind of screwball, fooling around in the theater. He walked out on me during rehearsal once."

"Why?"

"He kept asking me to come in sooner with my lines and I just couldn't. I mean, you can't deliver a line that way, not on order. Muni is the star, but I'm not about to get on that stage in front of an audience just to feed him lines. Muni flipped his lid and hollered, 'Damn it, you can drive trucks through the spaces between the cues!' He stomped offstage and Luther went after him. In a little while, Muni came back and he was just as sweet as could be. I don't know what Luther said to him, but whatever it was, it sure worked."

Later, I learned that Adler had managed to convince Muni that the inexperienced young actor would improve as he went along and that he, personally, would guarantee an impas-

Marlon, Paul Muni, and Celia Adler.
(GRAPHIC HOUSE, INC.)

sioned performance from him. Marlon wasn't a Jew, he explained, but he had embraced their cause with the fervor of a zealot. That was a little exaggerated, but it placated Muni and he returned to continue the rehearsal.

Marlon's troubles with Muni didn't end when the play opened. During its early run, he confided to me one day, "Freddie, you know that scene where Muni dies on stage? Well, at the beginning I'd cover him with a flag—body, face and all—and I'd stand over him, deliver my final speech, pick up a banner and march offstage to a crescendo of music. But Muni came up to me backstage the other day and suggested that I cover only his body, not his face. It would be more dramatic, he said, if the features of the old, dead Jew were seen while I made my speech.

"I agreed with him, but in the next performance I forgot all about his suggestion and covered him completely, face and all. I began my big speech, and when I looked down I saw the flag crawl down his forehead, slip away from his eyes along the bridge of his nose, slowly exposing his face inch by inch. It was like magic, and I was fascinated. The play flew right out of my head, of course, but I continued the speech with the muscles of my face.

"I saw Muni's upstage hand, the one hidden from the audience, pulling down the flag by gathering folds in his fist. The old hambone couldn't stand not having his face in the final scene. I was afraid I'd break up, so I stopped in the middle of the speech, kneeled, pulled the flag away from his face and tucked it tenderly under his chin. His expression was beatific. Imagine! He was supposed to be dead, but he was still acting. If the curtain hadn't come down, he'd have acted out all the stages of *rigor mortis* setting in. Man, what a ham!"

Ham or not, and in spite of the fact that the play was both

condescending and boring, it found a sympathetic audience and ran for 127 performances. In some ways, it was a breeze for Marlon. He used little or no makeup for his role and often wore his stage costume outdoors. When the final curtain fell and the actors had taken their bows, Marlon would walk straight from the stage to the street.

He was beginning to be known wherever he appeared, or at least he was in some quarters, and if he was not known, people looked at him anyway because he was so handsome. Yet I often heard people say, then and later, that he wasn't really handsome—ruggedly good-looking, perhaps, but not movie-star handsome. When people said that, I thought, What do they mean by "handsome"? If it means a face that captures and holds your attention, then Marlon was certainly handsome. Even when he was an unknown, wherever we went—restaurants, parties, on the subways—people would lower their newspapers to stare at him and stop whatever they were doing for a moment to gape at him unabashedly.

Sometimes I'd look at him and wonder what it was that caught the glances of passing strangers. In those days he had a straight nose, rounded at the end; a pouting, crooked mouth; small, pale-blue, narrowed eyes; a forehead that was too high and too broad, with a flattened lump over his right eye; and his blond hair was prematurely thinning out. There was nothing singular about his features, nothing remarkable about any one of them. Yet, put together as they were, they made Marlon Brando an exceptionally handsome man.

Once Marlon caught me staring at him and said, "What are you gaping at?"

"At your face," I said.

"What about my face?"

"You've got one of the most interesting faces I've ever seen," I said.

[79]

Marlon didn't know how to accept compliments then. Even if they were given sincerely by old friends, they made him shy and awkward. He would say or do some outlandish thing to cover up his embarrassment. In response to my compliment, for example, he suddenly went swishy and with sibilant s's began to sing Coward's "Mad about the Boy."

In those days, I must say, and for a long time after, I never had the feeling when I was with him that I was hobnobbing as a close friend of a celebrity. I thought of him as a pal, someone I'd been with since the days in Sayville. I was aware, of course, that he was a fine actor, but I had no idea that he was going on to the heights in his profession.

Marlon wasn't aware of who he was, either, for a long time. I remember once when we were staying in Berlin, while he was filming *The Young Lions*, well on into his career, and while we were having breakfast one morning, a commotion broke out in the street below. We went to the window and looked down from our tenth-floor room. Traffic was stopped in the street below by a huge mob that overflowed the sidewalk from curb to curb.

"My God, what's going on?" Marlon said. "Do you think the place is on fire?"

It took him a while—and some explanations from the desk —to realize that all those people were jammed up outside because they had heard he was in the hotel. He was stunned when he understood it, but he thoroughly enjoyed it later when his limousine moved slowly through the adoring fans.

So if it was true that I didn't think of Marlon as anything but a guy who had struck it lucky—neither did he.

CHAPTER SEVEN

I TOLD MARLON all about Vicki—that I was falling in love with a girl I really didn't care about except in a sexual way. "Every time I leave her," I said, "I swear I'm never going to see her again. But after a couple of days, she's all I think about, and I run to her like a lost child to its mother."

"When a chick has you by the balls," Marlon advised me, "it's no use trying to fight it, because you can't win. You'll have to play it out to the end. Let it run its course, or it'll get worse. But what should really worry you is this junk thing. You made a big mistake taking that first fix. Man, how could you stick a needle in your vein and shoot that poison into your system? Are you crazy? Or what?"

"That's the last time I'll ever do anything like that again," I said. "I can promise you that."

Promises, promises. Next time I saw Vicki, her dope connections, Joe and Claire were with her, and sure enough, the moment they offered to turn us on some smack, I accepted as though I had never made the resolution to refuse. In fact, I was anxious to turn on, to feel the flash, followed by the calming, warming effect, and I also knew how pleasurable sex with Vicki would be while I was under the influence. I was certain I'd never get hooked on the stuff. Like so many others, I was convinced that I was different, that I'd turn on only once in a great while. I might become a "joy-popper," but I'd never become a junkie. No, not me.

To shorten a long and familiar story, within a year I was a full, flat-out junkie. After living in a small apartment in the Village, Vicki and I broke up. In the beginning, heroin had enhanced the pleasures of sex, but when I got hooked I became impotent as well. I preferred the flashes induced by injecting heroin mainline to sexual climaxes. My grades at school took a nose-dive, and I quit. To support my ever-increasing habit, I took to stealing. I hustled around the city, shoplifting, working most of the shops on Fifth Avenue, taking awful chances of getting busted to get the price of a bag of dope. My habit cost me about fifty dollars a day, every day. There are no holidays on junk.

I used to score in Spanish Harlem on 110th Street and Fifth Avenue. The street was a bedlam of kids playing stickball, jukeboxes blaring Spanish music, small-time gamblers and ten-dollar hookers smoking marijuana in doorways, always on the alert for a live one.

After I scored, I'd walk around the corner to one of the

old, dilapidated hotels on Central Park North and tip the room clerk to use the bathroom. Occasionally, when I was flush, I'd buy him a carton of Camels. In the john, I'd quickly measure out a portion of heroin into a spoon, cook it, and so on, tie up, and mainline it. Sometimes the stuff was good, and sometimes it was weak. You never knew until it hit you. When it was good, I'd sit on the toilet seat and go on the nod. Once in a while I'd lose track of time and the clerk would rouse me with a loud rapping on the door. "Are you all right? Hey! Are you all right?" I'd pull myself out of my stupor and call through the door, "Yeah, I'm all right. I'll be out in a minute." When his footsteps faded down the hall, I'd clean up, wrap my works, and leave.

Every day I'd wake up alone in my room, take my morning fix, go to the shops to steal, score for my dope, return to my room, fix, go on the nod, and then to bed, day after day after day. What a life! What a waste!

I never saw him, of course, but Marlon was occasionally in Harlem in those days, although on much more innocent errands. It was safe to walk around in those happier days, and Marlon went there mostly because he loved black girls. He also liked to play bongo drums in any café band that would let him sit in. One night, he told me, he was in a place on Seventh Avenue, very dim, so dim the black patrons in it looked even blacker, and I suppose he looked even whiter by contrast, as the only honky there.

There was a trio playing, and after Marlon had a drink at the bar, he went over to the stand, flashed a wad of money, and asked if he could sit in and play the bongos. They let him, of course, and after the set, he went back to the bar for another drink. A black girl sitting there began to come on with him in a way that quickly led to Marlon's making arrangements with her to go somewhere and screw. Before they could leave, however, a large and powerful black man came up behind the girl, whirled her around, and hit her so hard that she flew against the wall.

Marlon said he thought there wasn't much point in waiting to see how it all came out. In fact, he fled out the door and began running for his life down the streets of Harlem. "Go, man! Go!" enthusiastic passers-by yelled at him as he sped past. He never looked back. If he had, he would have seen that nobody was chasing him.

In these crazy, early days, it seemed sometimes that almost anything could happen, and something happened to me in the midst of all my trouble. I met a girl named Marcia. She was living with a man I'll call Edward Locke, Jr., the son of an author who had written a best-selling book. Locke, Jr., seemed to be a very mild spastic, but worse, he was addicted to drugs and alcohol. Whether it was from these or his nervous condition, he appeared to have trouble with his coordination.

I met Marcia casually at the famous old Village bar and restaurant, the San Remo. She told me she worked for *Women's Wear Daily*. At the moment I was in between bouts with my habit, looking suntanned and healthy. We hit it off right away and began talking like old friends. She said she wanted to be a fashion editor. At the moment, she was struggling, living with Locke, and so poor that on the previous Christmas, she said, they had gone down to the Bowery and sold a couple of pints of blood for five dollars each so they could afford to buy Christmas dinner. I liked Marcia at once. She was not pretty in a conventional sense, but she had a fine figure and a certain kind of authentic style, and obviously she was intelligent. Adversity had given her a nervous manner.

Marcia told me that she wanted to break up with Locke but didn't want to hurt his feelings. Soon after I met her, he took an overdose of sleeping pills. She couldn't revive him and had to call the Fire Department, whose experienced crewmen brought him around. Thinking it was a suicide attempt, the police took him to Bellevue. Under the rules in those days, he would have been kept under observation for only a few days, usually ten, but the doctors had some doubts about his mental condition. So they kept him for sixty days. During that period, Marcia and I saw a lot of each other and fell in love.

Edward was still a complication, although Marcia said she wanted to leave him. He had been working with a young writer, getting Billy Rose's syndicated column together every day. The writer did most of the work. Edward could never get going until the deadline approached, and then he often got on pills and missed the deadline altogether. Naturally, he lost his job. Marcia was supporting him, but then she lost her own job. The relationship was ending even before he went to Bellevue.

Marcia came to live with me in an apartment on Thirty-second Street, near Fifth Avenue. She had determined not to tell Edward until he was out of the hospital and well again, but when she did, surprisingly he gave her no trouble. He simply took it in stride, then went right back on pills and alcohol.

I wasn't any better. I soon went back on junk, hooked again. Marcia didn't leave me, though, and eventually she met Marlon, who came around to call. She couldn't stand him, and she resented any time I spent with him. "You quarrel with him so often," she complained, "and he seems to want some kind of control over you." I put it down to jealousy.

Before things got too sticky, however, the three of us did spend some time together. He was there at our place one night when he said, "Freddie, let's go see Wally."

He meant Wally Cox, of course. Wally was one of Marlon's friends and remained a friend until his death. They had been in elementary school together, had played together, teased each other, and like the others who knew him in those days,

Wally called Marlon "Bud." Marlon once told me that when they were eight or nine, he had tied Wally to a tree one day while they were playing cowboys and Indians, and gone home, leaving him there. About suppertime came a call from Wally's worried family, and Marlon, conscience-stricken, hurried back to the tree. Wally was still there, making no effort to get free, calmly confident that someone would come and untie him.

Wally Cox had come to New York with his invalid mother and for a while had hustled to make a living, designing and making jewelry out of silver, but he couldn't get the business going. He wanted to be an actor, too, and he and Marlon had been students together at Elia Kazan's Actors Studio. He was often at Marlon's apartment on West End Avenue, and we all thought he was a sweet guy. He was the kind of man who seemed always like the meek, obliging Mr. Peepers he played in the television series that brought him success. If Marlon found that someone had forgotten to bring in any milk from the store, he'd ask Wally, "Would you mind running down and getting a little milk for us?" and Wally would go, obligingly.

Consequently, when Marlon suggested we go see Wally, I was a little bewildered and said, "Where?"

"He's at the Village Vanguard," Marlon said.

"What, as a bus boy?" I laughed.

"No, he's got an act there."

"Well, let's go then."

Marlon and Marcia and I stumbled down the steps of the Vanguard, which for so many years has been the home of good jazz and the launcher of numerous show-business careers. Wally was delighted to see us. He sat down at our table and talked with us before he went on. Marcia had to go to the john, and although it was time for Wally to be on stage, he wouldn't start until she came back. It was a great act, we thought, full of the quiet humor we knew him for when he was with us. I found out that he had been going to acting school and was writing his own material.

It was Marlon, I also learned, who had been responsible for getting Wally his start. He had been taking him to parties where agents and producers were present, and at the right moment he'd say casually, "Wally, do some of those things you do in class," and Wally would get up and do the turns with which he'd been amusing his fellow students at the Studio. When he was finished one night, an agent came up to him and said, "Do you think you can do that for money?" Wally allowed that he could and signed up.

That was how he had come to the Vanguard, where he was an instant success with the customers, who loved him. That led to an engagement which transported him from the Vanguard's cellar to the Rainbow Room's sixty-fifth-floor elegance in Rockefeller Center. There he made a new success in a show that included Betty Comden, Adolph Green, and Judy Holliday and became an overnight celebrity. His modest style overshadowed what he really did, because what he did was to change the whole style of American comedy from the stand-up one-liner to situations.

Just before all this transformed Wally's life, he was broke. I remember standing with him in a drugstore on Broadway one day, waiting to get into a phone booth so that I could spend the only dime I had in my pocket to call my connection and plead with him for some credit. Wally had a call to make, too, but I didn't want him to hear what would probably be a humiliating conversation, so I let him get ahead of me.

"Go ahead and make your call," I told him as someone came out of the booth. He started to move into it, and at the same time we saw on the shelf a handsome, thick, pinseal, gold-trimmed wallet. Before I could do anything, Wally pulled it out and held it high in the air, as though he were saying, "Look, I haven't even touched it yet."

"Let's look at it first, Wally, and see what's in it," I whispered feverishly. I was so desperate for money to get a fix that I had no scruples. But Wally paid no attention. He took the wallet over to the cashier, explained where he had found it, and started to walk away.

"Wait a minute," the cashier called. "What's your name?"

Wally turned around, surprised. The idea of a reward hadn't even occurred to him, but since he'd been asked, he gave his name and address. Sick and angry as I was, I could only look at him and think what a great human being he was.

Where Marlon was concerned, Wally was like family—in a class by himself among all the other Brando friends. He was the only one who dared to put Marlon down, dared to say calmly, "You don't know what you're talking about," when he was going on about something. In the days of his celebrity, Marlon would never have taken that kind of talk from anyone else.

I liked Wally very much, too, and might have seen more of him if he hadn't shot up to fame so suddenly and if I hadn't been fighting the habit and trying to stay with Marcia. We lived together for six years, but it couldn't work, at least not then. I was on and off junk, and she was beginning to do well in the world, first as fashion editor of *Photoplay* magazine and later in the same job on *Modern Bride*. She took me along on the parties she went to increasingly, parties where everybody was chic and uptown and full of admen's and PR men's talk and show-biz gossip. I'd sit there listening, often on the nod from the junk, but not being looked down on by the others because in those days there was something exotic about being a junkie. It gave you a kind of identity. But it gave Marcia more trouble, eventually, than she thought I was worth.

One night I came home and found my luggage in the hall and the door to the apartment locked. I pounded on it a little, knowing inside what was happening.

"Get out," Marcia yelled from inside. "Get out, or I'll call the police."

I couldn't blame her.

CHAPTER EIGHT

S O MUCH HAS BEEN written
about the circumstances that led to Marlon's being cast as
Stanley Kowalski in *A Streetcar Named Desire* that it would
be purposeless to discuss it further. Nevertheless, from the
viewpoint of one who saw it happen, there is an aspect of it
that may be useful to recall, if there is anyone left who doubts
that the element of chance plays a very large part in the destiny
of successful people.

To ensure the commercial success of *Streetcar*, Elia
Kazan, the director, wanted a box-office draw, a Hollywood
name, to play in a cast that was virtually unknown outside
the legitimate theater. He first offered the role of Stanley to

John Garfield, an established Hollywood star, who refused it on the grounds that the part was secondary to the Blanche Du Bois role. Kazan then offered the part to one or two other movie stars, who also refused it for the same reason.

Blanche Du Bois was certainly a character who dominated the play. Tennessee Williams' script called for a frail, aging beauty, blonde, very pale, dressed in gossamer—a moth attracted to the flame that would kill her. To play opposite her, for contrast, Kazan wanted a dark, masculine actor. Marlon didn't seem to fill the bill. He was blond, blue-eyed, and although he was powerfully muscular, he had a refined, sensitive face. Just the same, Marlon wanted the part. Kazan and Williams were skeptical, but they consented to have him read for them.

I've often heard it said that Marlon is a bad "cold reader," as they say in the theater, describing someone who comes in and reads for an audition. That rumor is untrue. He can read as well, if not better, than any actor who reads a script aloud for the first time. From the beginning he believed, and correctly, that it is only self-defeating to try to perform when you are not familiar with the material. But when you're a young actor, unknown and ambitious, and a good part comes along, you have to make compromises and take your chances. So Marlon read for Williams, who was astonished at the grasp he had of the character in the first reading. At the end of it, Williams said he wanted Marlon for the part.

Both Kazan and Williams were to get a surprise they hadn't counted on, however. During rehearsals, as Marlon experimented and searched for the character of Stanley Kowalski, the relatively secondary role began to loom larger and larger, until it seemed that it might dominate and overwhelm the stage. Kazan was afraid such a powerful performance would tilt the balance of the play, and he called Williams

The leads in the play A Streetcar Named Desire, *Karl Malden, Jessica Tandy, Kim Hunter, and Marlon.* (FRIEDMAN-ABELES)

to come in to watch a rehearsal. Naturally, the playwright was delighted when he saw it, to see the role he had written come to life on the stage. He had a brief conference with Kazan, and they decided to give Marlon his head. It was a wise decision. As everyone now knows, he gave one of the greatest performances of his career.

I attended a rehearsal of *Streetcar*, and although the staging was still rough and they were playing under a work-light, without a set, I was transported by the realistic acting and atmosphere of the play.

They were rehearsing the rape scene, and when Marlon entered, I got a shock. Without help of makeup or costume, my sweet, gentle friend had been able to transform himself into a monster. He had put that pelvis-thrust-forward slouch of his to good use and turned his petulant pout into a snarl. His T-shirt disclosed the heavily muscled torso of a truck driver, he mumbled like a moron, he scratched his asshole, digging in deep to get at the itching, and to show that he had a perpetual hard-on, he wore tight jeans to outline the bulge of his genitals. His impersonation of a complete brute was so perfect that I couldn't help but giggle.

Then I began to feel the need of a fix, and sneezed. Kazan turned around and spotted me in the last row, slouched down and trying to make myself invisible. He asked me who I was. Marlon spoke up and told him that I was his friend and that he had invited me to observe the run-through. Kazan politely asked me to leave. It was not a good policy, he said, to have a play seen while it was still in rough shape. I apologized and left.

Later, on the street, Marlon asked me, "Well, what do you think?"

"Fantastic," I said. "The play is bound to be a hit."

"Yeah," he said. "I think we've got something good going." Then, with his characteristic abrupt change: "I'm starving. Let's get a burger. I found a new joint, a real Sloppy Joe's."

I had to get away to hustle up some bread to score for dope. I was sneezing and nauseous, and my bones were beginning to ache, and if I didn't fix soon, I'd begin throwing up.

Marlon saw my teary eyes, my runny nose, and the grimace of agony on my face, and said, "Oh, man, when are you going to kick that shit? When you die from an overdose? Is that it? Do you want to die?"

"I don't want to die," I said. "I just don't want to go crazy. And junk keeps me from flipping out. That's what it is."

"Why don't you see a psychiatrist?"

"I'm too sick for that. In time, I'll know when to quit. There's a time for everything, and there'll be a time for kicking, too."

"Anything I can do?" Marlon asked.

I was tempted to ask him for some money to score, but I restrained myself. It would have put him in a bad spot. Knowing how generous he was, I was sure he wouldn't refuse me, but I also knew that he hated the idea of giving me money for dope.

"No," I said, "there's nothing you can do. I've got to run now. Later."

Marlon tilted his head to one side, gave me a sad, twisted smile, and said, "Later."

I didn't see him for several weeks after that, but while I was having coffee at Joe's Dinette on West Fourth Street one day, I opened the evening paper and saw that *Streetcar* was having a premiere that night. I'd forgotten all about it, lost in my own miseries.

It was nearly eight o'clock as I read and absorbed this information. The curtain would be going up in about forty minutes, and I could picture Marlon in his dressing gown, nervous, scared, preparing to make his entrance on stage. I wanted to give him a word of encouragement, but there was nothing I could do. It was too late to phone him, and besides, when an actor is that close to a premiere on Broadway, he can hardly relate to anyone or anything except the approaching ascent of that curtain. I could send a telegram, though, and hope it would be delivered on time. Those were the days when you could entertain a hope like that.

Marlon, Kim Hunter, and Jessica Tandy.
(GRAPHIC HOUSE, INC.)

I had only a dollar and a little change, scarcely enough to cover the cost of a telegram, so I sent him the shortest one I could think of, avoiding the flowery best wishes an actor usually gets, which I knew Marlon hated. My wire said: "Try not to make an ass of yourself. Good luck. Freddie."

The reviews next day were sensational; the play was a huge success. Overnight, tickets to *Streetcar* were very hard to come by. If you didn't know someone with influence, you wouldn't have the privilege of buying a couple of seats.

A few weeks later, after his evening performance, I went backstage to Marlon's dressing room. His first girl friend, Maria Lorca, was there. It was a long way from that summer in Sayville, but Maria had not changed. She was several years older than Marlon and was always sensible and proper in her behavior, never wild or uninhibited. Intimate as they were, he always treated her with the sort of courtesy that was near formality, and so did I—so did we all.

"Your telegram cracked me up," Marlon said. "I was nervous and tense, and it made me laugh, and I relaxed." His face reflected that opening-night amusement as he spoke, but Maria, who had been with Marlon when he got the telegram and in fact had read it to him, didn't share his humor. Her face was without expression and her eyes blank.

Marlon's own face suddenly changed expression, as though he had had a second thought, a doubt about something, and he said, "Did you *know* your telegram would have that effect on me? Did you send it spontaneously, or was it calculated?"

I thought, Now what difference does it make to him? And what a word to use, "calculated," as though I were in a conspiracy against him.

"I gave it some thought," I said. "I hoped it would hit you as it did. I'm glad it worked."

"Oh, I see," Marlon said, and a look of disappointment clouded his face.

What the devil was wrong? I wondered. Was there something sinister about the telegram and the spirit in which it was sent? I looked to Maria for some assurance, but she was no help. Her eyes were still empty and her expression neutral. The atmosphere in the dressing room became delicately brittle. Paranoia was in the air. I had taken enough heroin to last me for the night, but in spite of that, and although I wasn't sick, I felt that I could use another fix.

On the street, as we walked toward some restaurant or other, I decided I couldn't sit through dinner with them, wrapped in a mood so fragile it might, for some shadowy, incomprehensible reason, break into jagged shards about us. I stopped, told them I wasn't feeling very well, and had to leave immediately. Solemnly we said good night, and I walked away.

I could never figure out what happened that night. Marlon has never explained it.

One thing about seeing Marlon after his big success was to realize that he hadn't changed. Usually, when an actor succeeds after he has been poor and struggling, he raises his standard of living and changes his life style at least to some degree, but Marlon's success only appeared to make him funkier.

After a long run was assured, he moved to a furnished room with a communal bath down the hall in an old brownstone building on Fifty-second Street, right in the middle of the jazz joints, night clubs, tourist traps, posh restaurants, and greasy one-arm joints. His window opened on the liveliest, noisiest street in the world, and the sounds that drifted in at night seemed to infuse him with excitement. When he went to bed, the bustle lulled him to sleep like a baby.

The single large room was furnished with several mattresses strewn helter-skelter on the floor. There were no chairs, but lots of pillows to sit on. He acquired a hi-fi set which blared day and night. Then he bought bongo drums, boxing gloves, and a weight lifter's barbells.

As a final touch, he bought a used, powerful Indian motorcycle. We tooled all around town on that bike, Marlon always in Levi's and ratty tennis shoes, while I rode behind him

Marlon at one of his favorite pastimes.

properly dressed in shirt and tie. He was an expert driver, and I realized that it was really the most sensible means of transportation for him. He slithered through the snail-paced, bumper-to-bumper New York traffic like quicksilver and got where he wanted to go in a hurry.

In those days a rough-looking guy on a roaring motorcycle was a rare sight, and he attracted a hell of a lot of attention. Taxi drivers warned each other to be on the lookout for "a crazy kid on a motorbike who's looking to get himself killed."

Sometimes we'd drive through Central Park and he'd kick out the steel parking brace, so that when he banked on a sharp turn, the steel brace would scrape the asphalt drive and spray a dazzling arc of sparks high in the air as we zipped through the dark night.

Marlon insisted that I stay at his place one night, but I told him I couldn't because I needed to hustle up some bread for my morning fix. Marlon said he would give me the money to score, so I stayed.

Early the next morning I awoke, sick, desperately needing a shot. Marlon refused to give me the money he had promised me and tried to talk me into kicking my habit right then and there. He said he'd put me up at his place and take care of me and that he'd get a doctor for me if I should need one.

But I was much too sick even to consider kicking. My habit was far too big to break cold turkey, and I knew I would have to taper off. Marlon had hidden his money and wouldn't listen to my pleading. I searched frantically for it, but with no luck. Marlon watched me, studied me, while I was doing it, as though storing impressions for some future use. When he saw that my agony was truly unbearable, he got his wallet from its hiding place, put me on his motorcycle, and we tore uptown to Spanish Harlem so that I could score.

When we arrived there, the Puerto Ricans were fascinated

by the curious sight of Marlon and his motorcycle, and they crowded around him. He got panicky, and I told him I would be all right now and he could split, which he did.

I scored, shot up, and then indulged in some self-pity. I was at a loss to know how I could sink so low and wondered if I would ever pull myself out of my degradation.

Soon after, I decided to go home to my parents in Brooklyn and really try to kick the habit. About a week after I made the move, when the acute withdrawal symptoms began to subside, the doorbell rang. I answered and saw it was Marlon. I hadn't given my Brooklyn address to anyone, but somehow he had found me.

I didn't invite him in because I was ashamed of the poverty I lived in. He wanted to meet my mother and I brought her downstairs to him. My mother, Rosa, was a small, pretty woman, and Marlon, when he saw her, almost knelt in reverence. She was wearing a black silk scarf over her head, pinned at the chin, and a plain black coat. She looked like a saint.

Marlon hemmed and hawed and blushed and didn't know what to say except that he was happy to meet her. My mother didn't understand a word of English except when it was spoken within the family and scrambled with Italian, but she understood Marlon's awkwardness and blushes and took them as a compliment to her. She thought he was an attractive, charming boy, and I translated for her. Then she excused herself and went back upstairs.

"Aren't you going to invite me up for coffee?" Marlon asked.

I told him the truth—that I was ashamed of the poverty and ashamed that I was ashamed, and so on.

"But I don't care," Marlon said. "I don't care about such things. You know that."

"I know you don't care, but I *do*," I said.

"I've been riding my bike for hours," Marlon said. "You live on Jefferson *Street*, and I was searching for you on Jefferson *Avenue*, which is miles away, and it was hours before I found you. Come on, be a friend and invite me in."

"No. I won't ask you in no matter what you say. But we can go to a cafeteria somewhere, and you can have coffee and rest yourself."

Marlon shook his head sadly, got on his bike, kicked off, and I climbed aboard.

We went to a workingman's cafeteria on Broadway and Myrtle Avenue and I watched him as he gratefully gulped down several cups of steaming hot coffee. It had been a warm, sunny afternoon, but it had turned cold in the evening. He was wearing a T-shirt and jeans, and it was a long drive from Manhattan to Brooklyn. He had been driving for hours to find me, and he looked tired and chilled. I felt a sudden flush of affection for him, and I had to swallow a lump in my throat and fight back the tears.

Marlon had a performance that night, and it was getting late. He had to leave. Sick as I was, he talked me into accompanying him to the theater. I climbed aboard the motorcycle with him, and he drove like a loon to the city. We roared up to the theater with no time to spare, parked in the red zone and leaped off. The theatergoers standing outside under the marquee looked down their noses at us, not realizing that, in a few minutes, the hoodlum on the motorcycle, dressed in the clothes he was wearing, would be on stage entertaining them with his portrayal of the brutal Stanley Kowalski.

Offstage in those days, he was anything but brutal. He wanted me to get psychiatric help and said he'd pay the bill. He recommended a doctor, and I went to him. Within a few weeks, I began to suspect that this psychiatrist was a charlatan, a suspicion that later proved true, and I quit. Marlon was disappointed and angry with me and urged me to find another doctor. I told him it was hopeless unless I really wanted treatment—wanted it enough to pay for it myself. Reluctantly, he agreed with me.

Meanwhile, *Streetcar* continued its triumphant run. In one part of the play, Marlon had a span of twenty minutes or so in which he did not appear on stage. It bored him to stand around doing nothing while he was waiting for his cue, and besides, his energy would flag. He didn't want to go on stage dragging his heels, and so he'd exercise to keep his heart pumping and his senses quick.

Whenever I was around, we'd go to the basement beneath the stage, put on gloves and box. He'd always promise to pull his punches, but when the action got slow and he wanted to step it up, he'd hit me with a strong hook to my liver that would sink me to my knees. Enraged, I would try to retaliate with a couple of roundhouse rights to his chin.

"Not in the face! Not in the face!" he'd say, then throw a straight, stiff job into my nose. He was strong and fast, but he carried his left glove too low, exposing himself to an overhand right to his chin. I was often tempted to take advantage of this mistake and knock him on his ass, but I held back because he still had several scenes to perform. Although the gloves were as big as pillows, a punch to the head would stun you and give you a numbing headache, often leaving you with a persistent ringing in the ears.

Whenever I wasn't around, Marlon would get Karl Malden, or one of the other actors, or anybody else who was available to box with him. One night I had a date for dinner with him, and when I arrived at the theater to pick him up, I was told that he was in the hospital with a broken nose. He had been knocked over a crate while he was boxing with someone. The cast, performing on stage, had heard the loud crash, paused for a moment in wonder at what might be happening, then had gone on with the performance. When Marlon entered on cue with his nose gushing blood, the cast was horrified. Peculiarly enough, the audience seemed to be unaware that anything was wrong. Marlon managed to stick it out to the final curtain, then he was rushed to the hospital.

When I visited him there, his eyes were swollen and blackened, and his nostrils were packed with bloody gauze. He told me how it had happened.

"Nobody wanted to box with me," he said. "I saw the fireman standing around, doing nothing, so I asked him to go a couple of rounds with me. He was a shy kind of guy and wouldn't do it, but I kept goading him. I promised him that I'd only protect myself and wouldn't hit back. He said it was against regulations but he'd oblige me for a round or two.

"We put on the gloves, squared off, and circled each other, feeling each other out. All of a sudden, he winds up and throws a haymaker from the floor. I saw it coming, but I couldn't get out of the way. Next thing I knew I was flying ass over heels into a pile of wooden crates. I saw stars and I began bleeding from the nose like a stuck pig. The poor guy was afraid he'd killed me, but I told him I was all right and not to worry about getting into trouble. It would be a secret between us.

"I went to my dressing room and put some cold compresses on my beak, but I couldn't stop the bleeding. I heard my cue coming up and ran to make my entrance. I held my nose, but from the break in the bridge, a regular geyser of blood shot about ten feet across the stage. Jessica [Tandy] was petrified, and by the time we came to the end of the play, the stage was covered with blood. When the curtain came down, they rushed me here, and here I am. And you know, I'm kinda happy to be here. This long run is getting to be a fucking bore."

A few days later, Irene Selznick, the producer of *Streetcar*, visited Marlon to see if he was fit enough to resume his role. Box office receipts were falling because of his absence.

As a matter of fact, Marlon had healed rapidly. The swelling had gone down and his nose was no longer stuffed with gauze. A little makeup would cover the discoloration of his eyes, and he would look as good as new. But he was enjoying his rest in the hospital, and when he heard that Irene was coming to see him, he painted his nose, cheeks, and eyes with iodine, wrapped his head with several layers of gauze and surgical tape, and looked like a man dying of a fractured skull.

When Irene saw him, she almost dropped in a dead faint. "Oh, my poor, *poor* darling!" she cried. "What have they done to you?"

"It's nothing," Marlon said. "Nothing at all. I want to get back to work—tonight." And he made a heroic effort to get out of bed.

"I wouldn't *dream* of it," she said. "Now you get back in bed and stay there. I'd rather shut down the play than have your death on my conscience."

Marlon sighed and collapsed on the bed as though the struggle to rise had been too much for him. When his visitor left, he removed the bandages and got on the phone to call some broad to visit him for a couple of hot minutes.

The broken nose was badly set, and when the bandages were off, it had acquired a flattened look. The doctor suggested plastic surgery. Marlon asked me what I thought about doing it, and I advised him against the nose bob, out of my own bitter experience. "Always ask the man who owns one," I said.

As it turned out, the broken nose served him well in his career. A straight nose would have appeared out of place in that craggy face.

When he was back in the cast again, Jessica Tandy knocked on his dressing room door one night after a performance and called, "Marlon, are you decent? Someone wants to meet you."

"Please come in," Marlon shouted through the door.

When it opened, Jessica and another woman were standing on the threshold. They stepped in, and as Jessica was about to introduce her friend, Marlon interrupted, "Don't tell me. I know. She's your mother."

Marlon is terribly nearsighted, and because he always loses them, he almost never wears his glasses—unfortunately, this time. The other woman was Sheilah Graham, the Hollywood columnist, and Marlon's unlucky remark must have hit her like a small shock wave. As she herself has confessed in her books, Miss Graham is a little vain about her looks and a little touchy about her age. Marlon did the best he could. He apologized, saying he hadn't had a good look at her before he spoke, but she was obviously seething. She sat down stiffly in a chair, and without saying a word about whether she had liked his performance or not, she began to ask rather abrupt, perfunctory questions about his career.

"Why have you refused the offers to come to Hollywood, Mr. Brando?" she wanted to know.

"Well, uh, well, I don't know, really," Marlon admitted. "I haven't given it any serious thought, I guess."

He never liked giving interviews to reporters, particularly Hollywood gossip writers, and avoided them whenever he could, as though they had contagious diseases. To find himself being interviewed, without his consent, by an irate female journalist who addressed him in terms of pure ice knocked him far off base.

But Marlon was too shy at that point in his career to express his feelings about such infringements on his privacy.

He shifted from foot to foot, trying to stifle his anger as he parried her questions. After a while, Miss Graham rose from her chair, still plainly indignant, and left. In her next column she wrote that she was glad to know Marlon wouldn't come to Hollywood because there were more than enough temperamental actors who delayed shooting schedules and skyrocketed production costs.

Temperamental? I thought when I read the column. How could she have possibly come to the conclusion, on the basis of one brief interview, that Marlon was temperamental? But that, as I learned later, was Hollywood.

What Miss Graham didn't know was that Marlon had already been to Hollywood for a screen test and that the executives in the front offices had decided his hair was thinning, his nose was bent, and his acting ability only fair. If Brando agreed to have his nose straightened and his name changed, they said, they would sign him to a seven-year contract with six-month options. Upon hearing this, Marlon had instructed his agent to tell them they could shove their seven-year contract with six-month options up their ass. He hopped a plane back to New York, giving Hollywood at least a figurative middle-finger salute as he departed.

OPPOSITE: *Jessica Tandy and Marlon.* (GRAPHIC HOUSE, INC.)

CHAPTER NINE

A<small>T LAST</small> *Streetcar* came to the end of its long run, and Marlon prepared to depart for his first visit to Europe. He hated flying and consequently decided to take a ship to France. A small group of friends gathered in his cabin to see him off. Reading the label on the bottle of champagne chilling in an ice bucket, and seeing that it was French, Marlon said, "Let's drink this before it becomes domestic." We popped the cork, made a toast, and wished him *bon voyage*.

In a month or two he was back, full of amusing stories about his European adventures. Some time before the trip he had seen *Les Enfants du Paradis*, and it had become one of his favorite movies. Arletty, the French actress who starred in it, had so enchanted him that one of his first acts when he got to Paris was to arrange a meeting with her. It was a disaster. "Boy, was I disillusioned," Marlon said. "She turned out to be a real tough bird." She had played Blanche Du Bois in the French stage version of *Streetcar*, which Marlon went to see. He admired her performance, but he told me that the actor who had played Stanley was a laugh.

"To show anger," he said, "this joker kept leaping over furniture. Over tables, chairs, and things. It made me and the audience a little jumpy."

In Italy, he had done most of his traveling on trains. On the way to Rome, he found himself installed in a tiny compartment with foldaway conveniences. That is, you raised a cover and a washbasin was revealed, another concealed a toilet bowl, still another was a drawer for your luggage. Waking in the middle of the night in urgent need of a bowel movement, he hadn't been able to find the light switch, and, in the dark, pulled up what he thought was the cover of the toilet bowl and relieved himself. In the morning, he discovered that he had taken a shit on his luggage.

At the station in Rome, when he tried to get a taxi, all the drivers held their noses and put up their "occupied" flaps. Marlon walked down the long line of taxis and finally caught a driver napping. Desperate to get a ride, he sneaked into the cab, and, when he was safely inside, shook the driver awake.

"When the guy woke up and smelled the stench," Marlon said, "he was afraid to turn around to see what the hell had crawled into his cab, and he tried to pull his head in like a turtle."

Not long after Marlon's return, I was walking along Fifth Avenue one sunny afternoon when I saw Brando Senior and Dodie emerging from a taxi and stopped to chat with them. I

hadn't seen Dodie for some time, and the change in her appearance was a shock. She had put on weight, her hair showed some gray, her clothes were plain, and she wore a small straw hat. She told me that she was filling her time in Libertyville with amateur theatricals, social work, and a bit of gardening. I wondered what she grew in her garden. I didn't ask, but I guess I pulled a long face.

"I grow flowers, not potatoes," she said, smiling. "Good God, do I look that frumpy? No, don't answer that."

As for Brando Senior, he was in somewhat worse shape. Ironically, his fortunes had been declining while his son's were rising. But although he was a little down on his luck for the moment, he thought he would soon be riding high again. It was just a matter of the economy settling down after the war years, that was all. Just the same, I could see a growing doubt was in his mind. I supposed it was the first time he had been compelled to face the possibility of failure—failure of a permanent kind, the kind that breaks the spirit.

When I saw Marlon after that sidewalk meeting, I said, "What's your mother doing to herself?"

"What do you mean?" he said a little sharply.

"She looks like dear old Aunt Dodie from Dullsville."

"I think she looks great," Marlon said. "She never looked better. And I've told her so."

"But she's not ready for the porch and the old rocking-chair bit."

"I told you, I like her as she is now."

"Well, I don't. I liked her as she was. And as she was, she was great, drinking problem and all."

"Well, she's *my* mother, not *yours*," Marlon snapped. "And if you tell her about how you feel, I swear, I'll never speak to you again. I mean it."

[111]

OPPOSITE: *Marlon and Teresa Wright in his first film,* The Men. (UNITED ARTISTS)

Vivien Leigh and Marlon in his second film,
A Streetcar Named Desire. (WARNER BROS. PICTURES INC.)

I could see he did mean it, and of course I said nothing to Dodie.

Meanwhile, in this interval after *Streetcar*, Marlon was getting numerous offers to go to Hollywood. He could write his own ticket, and he could have had his choice of any number of hot properties. He chose to make his film debut in Stanley Kramer's *The Men*, in which he was to play a paraplegic. While the picture had honorable, noble intentions, it turned out to be a sentimental, tear-jerking soap opera—the usual Stanley Kramer horseshit. Its budget was small, but that didn't prevent it from bombing at the box office, deservedly, I thought.

I don't know what possessed Marlon to choose it for his first film, but as usual he played the part as he saw it and scored a personal success. If it did nothing else, however—and it didn't—the film answered one important question: Would Marlon be as good on film as he had been on stage? The answer was unequivocal. He was even better.

Yet the ultimate recognition was slow in coming. When the film version of *Streetcar* was up for the Academy Awards, Vivien Leigh, Karl Malden, and Kim Hunter won Oscars for their performances in it, and Elia Kazan won for directing it. But Marlon lost to Humphrey Bogart's performance in *The African Queen*. Except for Marlon, *Streetcar* made a clean sweep of the Oscars.

There were a good many people who thought that the Hollywood bigwigs had denied him the award out of vindictiveness. They were fond of recalling Marlon's well-publicized threat, "If I win the Oscar, I'll send a cab driver to pick it up for me," and not many doubted that he would do it. He had also been widely quoted in newspapers and magazines for his unflattering opinions about Hollywood and its people: "Producers have the manners of ants at a picnic." "Hollywood is a depot for neurotics." "I came to Hollywood because I lacked the moral courage to refuse the money." "Hollywood is a cultural boneyard." Those were only a few samples of his outspoken contempt for the business that would soon make a fortune for him.

I remember watching the Awards ceremony that denied Marlon what most people thought was his due. The audience, studded as usual with stars, producers, directors, and executives, gasped in audible disappointment when they realized that Marlon, who had been considered a shoo-in, had lost to

James Mason and Marlon rehearsing for Julius Caesar.

Bogart. That was unfair to Bogart, however, and this same audience appeared to realize it quickly. Brando may have deserved it, but the honor to Bogart was long overdue. He accepted the award graciously and walked off with the statuette, swinging it by its ankles with its head down, as though he were a carpenter carrying a hammer to repair something backstage. The audience loved it and gave him a thundering ovation.

Later I asked Marlon if he felt as though he had been cheated out of the Oscar. He thought for a while, shrugged his shoulders, and said, "Nope. The Oscar and all those other acting awards are a crock of shit. If they had given me the Oscar, I'd have used it as a doorstop."

Oscar or not, he was much in demand in Hollywood, and again the question was, what next? I found out "what next" in a manner as unorthodox as the ploy that got Marlon the part. One of the things I learned from him was to sit on the toilet seat while urinating. I learned it one day when he and I were in the bathroom in his apartment and he lowered his pants and sat on the bowl. I don't mind sharing a urinal with a chum and chatting with him while our bladders are emptying, but I won't stay in the john with him while he's defecating, so I started to leave.

"Where are you going?" Marlon said.

"I'm getting out of here," I said. "I don't want to be around anybody when they're taking a crap. It offends my aesthetic sensibilities."

"Your *what*? I didn't think wops *had* aesthetic sensibilities. Anyway, I'm not taking a crap, I'm taking a leak."

"Sitting down?" I said. "Girls sit. Men stand."

"Who says?"

"It doesn't need saying. We just happen to be built that way."

[115]

"Nonsense. Guys can piss from any position they please. Standing on their head, if they like. I got bored standing and watching myself pee. By the way, I just signed to do *Julius Caesar.*"

"You're too young to play Julius Caesar."

"I'm playing Marc Antony, birdbrain. Louis Calhern is playing Caesar."

"Oh," I said. "Who else is in the cast?"

"James Mason is Brutus. John Gielgud is Cassius, Deborah Kerr is Portia, and Greer Garson is Caesar's wife. Some lineup, huh?"

"I'll say. Top-drawer, first-rate, prime-cut, captain's table, and all that, matey."

"Yeah, yeah. And not bad, too. I've got top billing. And to think I almost didn't get the part. I had to audition for it."

"Audition? You mean screen-test, don't you?"

"No. I mean audition. I recorded a speech on tape for Mankiewicz. He played it for the guys in the front office, and I guess they liked it."

Then I found out how Joe Mankiewicz had done it. As producer-director of the picture, he had told the studio heads that he wanted Marlon for Marc Antony. They screamed bloody murder. They were convinced that Marlon was a mumbler, a mug who could never handle the Shakespearean dialogue. So Mankiewicz asked Marlon to tape record the "Friends, Romans, countrymen" speech, and then he got the studio heads together, played the tape for them, and asked them to name the actor. They named several—Laurence Olivier, Jose Ferrer, Maurice Evans, John Gielgud, and few other notable Shakespearean actors. Then Joe told them it was Brando. They made no further objections, and Marlon got the part.

Before he started work, however, he wanted to do a play using only his friends and to take it on the road. He chose

Shaw's *Arms and the Man,* planning to tour it through the New England summer circuit.

"Listen, playboy," he said to me, "how'd you like to come on the road and get your ass off the streets this summer?"

"Can I bring my connection along to keep me supplied with dope?"

"You hooked again?"

"Not quite. But almost. If I quit now, I'll have a few bad days, but that's all."

"I need a stage manager," he said. "I'll give you a small part, and you'll understudy the second lead. Think you can handle it?"

"Nope. I'll goof it for sure. You'd better get an experienced stage manager. Somebody you can rely on."

"That's not the point. I'm going on the road to fuck around and have some fun, and I don't want strangers hanging about. I'm taking Valerie Judd, Marie and Philip Rhodes, Janice Mars—the whole gang."

"Oh, I thought it was gonna be a big MCA deal." (The Music Corporation of America was Marlon's agent.)

"Shit, no. That's what I want to get away from, for a while."

"In that case, I'm your man. What's the play?"

"Arms and the Man."

"Why that? Why not some contemporary play?"

"I told you. I don't want to work. I want to fuck around. And I want to try comedy for a change. A farce. I want to leer, wear a mustache, make asides to the audience, like Groucho Marx."

So we went on the road, and although Marlon's attempt at comedy was disastrous, and even in spite of a slipshod production, we played to packed houses, who didn't seem to mind Marlon's performance. In comedy, his precise timing goes askew, his gestures become too broad, and the fact that he's "going for the laugh" is all too obvious.

As I write this, Marlon has not been able to carry off a performance in a straight comedy successfully. But oddly enough, off the stage and screen and among his friends, he is one of the funniest storytellers alive. Somehow, he simply can't translate his wit and humor onto the boards or films. I'd never write him off as a comedian, however. His genius is so unpredictable that he might, one day, disprove the old notion that comedians are born, not made.

After a summer that was pure fun, the tour came to an end, and I came back to the city and got hooked again. I overdosed too frequently, and I began to realize that if I didn't kick for good, I would soon be dead. I *wanted* to kick badly enough and believed I truly meant it this time, but I was broke and alone. Kicking cold turkey on the street is a long, hard way to go.

I knew that my constant demands on Marlon were beginning to strain our relationship, but there was no one else I could go to for help, and so I went to him and asked to borrow five hundred dollars. I promised it would be the last time I'd ever bug him about my drug problem. He had already told me that he'd never give me money for dope again, but if I really wanted to kick, he'd do all he could to help me.

"What do you really want the money for?" he asked me. "Tell me the truth. For dope?"

"No," I said. "I'm going to use the money to kick. But I've got to get away from the city—hole up some place away from drugs."

Marlon promptly loaned me the five hundred and told me to keep him posted on my progress.

To kick, I went to Fire Island, of all places. It was then not much more than a sort of seaside playground for the

ABOVE: *Some of the* Arms and the Man *touring company. Standing: William Redfield, Herbert Ratner (director), Janice Mars, Lydia Westman, and the author. Sitting: Ann Kimball, Marlon, Sam Gilman, and Phil Rhodes.* (EDWIN GRAY, FALMOUTH)

Janice Mars, the author, and Marlon in costume and makeup for Arms and the Man.

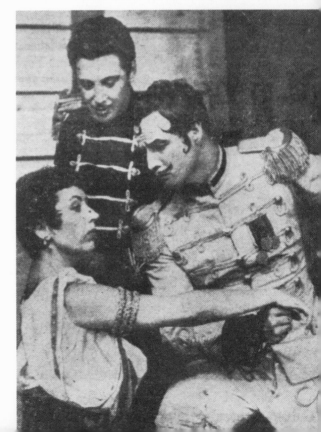

fashionable. It was pre-season, early in June, and the prices were skyrocketing. The going price for a room the size of a prison cell was fifty dollars a week, which was an awful sum in those days. Food, drink, tobacco, everything was over-priced. At that rate, the money Marlon had given me wouldn't last very long, so I decided to go elsewhere, maybe rent a cabin in the woods.

While I was waiting for the ferry out of Fire Island, I stopped for a cup of coffee at the Blue Bake Shop, a bakery where food was also served, specializing in breakfasts. The shop was owned and managed by two old German women. One of them was a circus performer "in the old country," as she said, and although she was seventy years old, she could still turn a cartwheel and walk on her hands. This elderly acro-bat—I'm sorry to say I've forgotten that sweet lady's name—sat with me for a chat, and I told her about the trouble I'd been in trying to find a room I could afford.

"Have you ever worked as a waiter?" she asked me.

"Yes," I said, "I've been a waiter."

"It's going to be very busy when the season begins, and I'll need a waiter. Would you consider working here? I'll give you a room and your meals and a small salary. With tips, you'll make out all right. Do you want it?"

"Yes," I said. "I want it."

"When you finish your coffee, I'll show you to your room."

I drained my cup, picked up my suitcase, and followed her to the rear of a shop. The neat, airy room she showed me con-tained a chair, a dresser, and a small, comfortable-looking bed.

Customers were few, but the work was still more than I could handle. I was suffering withdrawal symptoms and my nerves were raw. When I served coffee, the cups rattled in my grip. The German lady began to worry that I couldn't manage the job. She wanted to hire another waiter, a student perhaps, to help me. I assured her that I would soon be fully recovered from my illness (I'd told her that I had a minor liver ailment, to explain my extreme slimness and junkie pallor) and before long the work would be a breeze.

It was true. I gained strength every day, and within a week or so I was a fair waiter, getting generous tips from the customers who jammed the shop during week-ends. In the middle of the week, when business was light, I'd swim in the sea, lie in the sun, and go for solitary walks along the shore. In that healthy, invigorating atmosphere, it was hard to believe that I'd ever use junk again.

I didn't need the money I had borrowed from Marlon. Within a month, when I was secure in my job, I bought a postal order for five hundred dollars and sent it off to Hollywood. Marlon was happy to hear about my good luck, told me to stay straight until he got back to New York, and then he'd try to place me in some job or other.

A summer dream. When I got back to the city in the fall, it was the old story all over again. Before I knew it, I was hooked again. It happened so quickly I was stunned. One fix, and I was off and running.

When he got into town and saw me, Marlon was deeply disappointed. He had been as certain as I was that at last I'd shaken the habit. But even though I had failed him, he kept his promise and gave me a job, as his stand-in for *On the Waterfront*, which he was beginning to shoot in Hoboken, New Jersey. So began a new phase of our long relationship.

CHAPTER TEN

W

HILE WE WERE filming,
Marlon kept me beside him all the time, and I shared the
luxuries accorded only to movie stars and Very Important
People. That was lucky for me because the weather was freez-
ing on the Hoboken waterfront location, and the supporting
actors, the crew and technicians, although they were wrapped
in layers of heavy clothing, gathered around the fires blazing in
garbage cans in order to warm themselves. They crowded over
the flames, sipped coffee out of paper cups, and stamped their
feet to prevent frostbite. Working outdoors without respite,
the crew thrust their hands, gloved in cold, stiff leather, directly
into the flames to thaw and dry them.

Marlon and I, on the other hand, would hurry to the hotel about a block away, go to his room, remove our shoes and socks and paddle our feet in the scalding water that splashed into the tub. He'd call room service and order steak, baked potatoes, hot apple pie, and coffee for two. Then we'd lounge in the steam-heated room, our stomachs full, enjoying the warmth until the second assistant would appear in the doorway, red-nosed and shivering, to tell Marlon they were set up and ready for him.

Kazan, who was directing the picture, was a glutton for work. He seemed never to tire, and his enthusiasm never flagged. I figured he had to stoke himself with an extraordinary amount of fuel to produce so much drive, yet I'd never heard him order anything for lunch but a breast of chicken on toast, with no butter or mayonnaise, and a cup of tea. I wondered where he got his energy, and I asked him if he ever got tired, like ordinary people.

"I never get tired making a film," he told me. "I could go all day and all night. But at a cocktail party, listening to all that genteel bullshit, I'd collapse from fatigue within a half hour."

Sam Spiegel was the producer of the picture. It was said of him that he could be placed in a foreign country without a stitch of clothes, and although nude and unknown, in twenty-four hours he would be magnificently tailored, living in the penthouse suite in the best hotel in town, and traveling in a chauffeured limousine. He was an absolutely dazzling con man.

On location, late one dismal night, when the crew was half dead with cold and fatigue, Mr. Spiegel, wearing a great-coat with a luxurious collar of thick dark fur, stepped out of a sleek limousine, flanked by two stunning high-fashion models. He scanned the location, searching for Kazan.

Nobody seemed to be working. That was because Kazan

*The author and Marlon clowning on location during the
filming of* On the Waterfront.

hated visits from producers; he said they put him off his stride. He had devised an ingenious ploy to get rid of them. Whenever one stepped on the set, he ordered all work to stop, giving the men a coffee break of indefinite duration, and telling them they would be called when they were needed. On this particular night, he had apparently seen Spiegel coming from afar, or been warned that the visit was imminent, because nothing was going on.

When Spiegel saw the crew idle and his money as good as flushed down the toilet bowl, he became exceedingly agitated, storming at Kazan for dismissing the men and demanding an explanation for the delay. Kazan explained calmly that he would be a poor host indeed if he did not give his producer his undivided attention when the executive visited him. I don't know whether Spiegel was convinced or not, but he got his business done in a hurry, packed his pretty models back into the limousine, and sped away to resume his busy life in the city.

Everybody remembers the famous cab scene in *Waterfront*, with Marlon and Rod Steiger, and that memorable line, "I cudda been a contender. I cudda been *somebody* instead of a bum—which is what I am." As it happened, this scene was filmed indoors at an uptown studio, five minutes away from my junk connection.

Marlon was dissatisfied with the way the scene was going, and he had interminable quarrels with Kazan and Spiegel. During one of these "private discussions," I slunk away to score, believing it would take me only fifteen minutes or so. It was more than an hour later when I got back, and I was stoned. I saw Marlon sitting in the cab, standing in for himself, while Boris Kaufman, the cinematographer, was adjusting the lighting.

I went to Marlon and said, "I'm sorry. My connection hung me."

"I know, I know," he interrupted. "Spare me the details."

"Listen, man, if I'm bugging you, just let me know. I don't need this job. I can always go back to stealing."

Marlon smiled. "No, man, I'm bugged about something else. It's this fucking scene. Something's wrong with it, and I can't figure out what. So I sat here trying to pluck something out of the atmosphere. And so far—nothing."

"I watched the rehearsal," I said. "It wasn't perfect but it seemed to play passably well. If that's any help to you."

"Yeah, sure. It's a lot of help," he said. "With that and a nickel I could get a ride on the Staten Island ferry. Any other suggestions, genius?"

"Yeah," I said. "Now that you mention it, the gun-pulling bit hits a bullshit note."

Marlon's interest immediately picked up. "What do you mean?"

I told him that when he expressed fear of being shot by Rod Steiger, his fright seemed a little false. After all, Steiger, although a gangster, was still his brother, and shocked disbelief that his brother would pull a gun on him seemed a more appropriate reaction than fright. I had unwittingly hit on the same complaint that Marlon had been making about the scene, and he flipped his lid.

"That's exactly what I've been saying about this fucking scene all along," he said. He jumped out of the cab and pretty soon he and Kazan and Spiegel were closeted in one of the stormiest conferences I had ever heard, judging by the sounds that emerged.

I was sitting in the cab, and while Kaufman was lighting the scene, Kazan emerged from the conference room and crossed to me. He put his hand gently on my knee and said, "Did you say anything to Marlon about this scene?"

"Yeah," I said.

"What did you say?"

"I made a suggestion about the gun bit."

"Listen, kid," Kazan said, "do me a favor, huh?"

"Yeah, sure."

"Next time you get an idea about a scene, bring it to *me*, not to Marlon, okay? Huh?"

"Yeah, sure," I repeated.

"Thanks, kid. It'll save a lot of trouble," he said. Then he patted my knee and walked away.

I hated being talked to in that way and hated being called "kid." But Marlon was my friend, and I knew that he'd insisted I stand-in for him over many protests. My loyalty belonged to him, not to Kazan or anyone else. I decided then and there that whenever I thought I had a constructive suggestion, I would offer it to Marlon immediately. And if anybody didn't like it, or complained about it, that was too bad. They could lump it.

While we were filming *Waterfront*, Dodie came over to Hoboken and visited him on the set. Once again she was the slim, chic woman I had known. I supposed she was drinking again, but so what? You never saw her drunk, or smelled liquor on her breath. She was never loud or impolite, and she never slurred a word—or a friend.

It was a drizzly day when she visited, and we were shooting on the tar roofs of the waterfront tenements. Dodie and I found shelter under a canvas lean-to, smoked cigarettes and talked of old times. She was so easy to be with, so charming, and she laughed so readily at my jokes, that I almost fell in love with her again. But although she seemed so calm and

Eva Marie Saint, in her first picture, with Marlon.
(COLUMBIA PICTURES)

*Ex-fighter Tony Amato, Marlon, and the author on a
rooftop in Hoboken.* (COLUMBIA PICTURES)

collected, she appeared to me to be very insecure, and I thought I knew why.

What role was she to play now? Could that have been what was going through her mind? I wondered. She could play the old-fashioned mother to her son, now so successful in his career. Or she could be the lover-mistress-wife to her husband, who was failing. If that was truly her dilemma, her death not long afterward solved it. On this rainy day under the lean-to, I could only feel terribly sorry and immensely charmed.

Kazan was rushing to get all of Marlon's scenes in the film completed because Brando was due in Hollywood very soon to begin making another film, *The Egyptian*; and if he was delayed because of *Waterfront*, Spiegel would have to pay a heavy indemnity.

It was about three in the morning when Kazan shot Marlon's final scene. When it was called a "wrap," everyone, crew and all, broke into spontaneous applause. After we had said our good-byes and Marlon and I had walked away some distance, Kazan shouted after him, "Don't forget to wet your lips when the camera starts to roll."

We took the Hudson Tubes to New York. Marlon was wearing his dockworker's costume and was still in makeup, so the few early-morning riders who glanced at us didn't recognize him. We walked down the aisle and stood on the platform behind the cars. Marlon was silent, preoccupied about something.

"What's the matter?" I asked.

"I'm having trouble with Movita," he said.

I had no trouble believing it. Movita was a Mexican actress whom Marlon had met while he was in New Mexico making *Viva Zapata!* She had visited the set, he had taken one look at her dark, exciting beauty, always the kind he liked, and they were in bed together before the day was over. At the time we were making *Waterfront*, she was living with him in New York in an apartment across from Carnegie Hall. Marlon had taken a large dance studio on the top floor and made it into a bachelor apartment. The place was always in a terrible mess—ripped couches, worn linoleum, all kinds of things strewn around.

Movita was as full of superstitions as a gypsy, but when it came to sex she was extremely practical. She could measure a man's penis by his hands, so she said. Marlon's hands were strange, and he didn't like them; they were like the hands of a syphilitic dwarf, as he put it. But Movita didn't mind about that. She had a truly passionate sex life with him.

More than anything else, however, she wanted to marry Marlon. She came to me in tears one day, wanting to know why I thought Marlon wouldn't marry her when she wanted to so much.

"What do you think is wrong?" she asked pleadingly. "I have done everything I could for him."

"I don't know," I said, trying to think of something. "He leads a kind of undisciplined life, you know. Maybe he wants a home."

That was enough for Movita. She went right out and spent $5,000 redecorating that beat-up Carnegie apartment. When I saw Marlon again, he said, "Jesus, what did you tell Movita?"

"I told her I thought you wanted a home."

"For God's sake. Don't you know that's just going to make it harder to say good-bye?"

But he did say good-bye (although in 1960 he would marry Movita) and shortly after began to go out with another Latin beauty, who was then playing bit parts in movies and later became a star. She was a sensual woman, and I didn't like her much, but then I never did like Marlon's women. I didn't like her, I guess, because she was such an ambitious girl, always coming on with his friends.

One night in Hollywood, she and Marlon were having some heavy sex in an apartment he had at the time on Laurel Canyon Drive, overlooking Sunset Boulevard. It was a hot summer night and the place wasn't air-conditioned, so they decided to continue their engagement on the roof, where it was cooler, taking their blankets and pillows with them. This girl was what is known as a screamer, meaning that in the ecstasy of intercourse she liked to yell obscene words and phrases. Ordinarily Marlon didn't object; reacting as most men would, it enhanced his image of himself as a great lover. But that night, on the roof, she began screaming in a way she hadn't

Movita and Marlon mugging in a photo booth.

done before. While the neighbors listened on that humid, breathless night, she cried out, "Fuck me, Marlon Brando! Fuck me, Marlon Brando!"

"My God," Marlon said, "not my name, you damn fool," and clamped his hand over her mouth.

Eventually, years later, Movita won her long struggle with Marlon by getting pregnant, which was the only thing that would get him down the aisle. He bought her a house and gave her an income, but he never lived with her. She bore him a son, and for that he was grateful. Some time ago, he divorced her.

So this was the kind of trouble Marlon meant he was having with Movitá, as we traveled back to New York that night from Hoboken, at the end of *Waterfront*. Consequently, I thought something worse must have happened several weeks later when, as I was walking along Broadway, I glanced at the newspapers displayed on a stand and read the banner headline BRANDO DISAPPEARS and the subhead "Foul Play Feared." I knew Marlon was back in town, but I hadn't seen him, so I bought a paper and hurried over to the Carnegie Hall apartment.

As I knocked, I noticed a mirror on the door which hadn't been there before. The door was opened only enough for me to slide in, like a conspirator, and I saw that the mirror was a see-through by which Marlon could examine his visitors. I knew he detested sensational publicity, and I asked him what the headlines were all about.

"Well," he said, "after I read the screenplay of *The Egyptian* and met the cast, I wanted *out*. The whole thing was so bad, so Hollywood bad, that I just couldn't do it. I told Zanuck that, and you wouldn't believe what he said. He said, 'Look at it this way, Marlon. You're in the trenches, see? And you've got to go over the top. You don't *want* to go over the

The happy couple out for an evening.

top, but you've *got to*, see? Do you understand?' Imagine! That rabbit-toothed failure of the one-arm chin-up gave me the old army routine. The stuff you feed the troops. So I went back to my hotel and packed. I left some things behind so they wouldn't think I'd split, but I split."

Zanuck was so certain Marlon would come back that for three days or so he kept the crew on the set, ready and waiting for him. When he realized that his star was gone for good, he closed down the set and sued Marlon for a million dollars. He had Brando by the short hair; the contract was ironclad. Marlon's lawyers advised him to come to some sort of settlement, and the suit was dropped when he agreed to star in *two* films for Zanuck. One of them was *Desirée*, in which he played Napoleon. The movie was no more than a perfunctory gesture to satisfy the agreement, as far as Marlon was concerned. "I used a lot of nose putty and layers of makeup and just walked through the part," he told me later.

The other picture, of course, was *The Young Lions*. Maybe he shouldn't have shown his anger about *The Egyptian* to Zanuck; at least he could have avoided *Desirée*. He was usually good at not showing it; his grandmother, he told me, had once told him never to show his anger at all, but wait and his time would come. But Marlon seemed to apply that advice best in his relationships with women. He never let a girl go in an honest way, if he was angry with her, or they had quarreled. He waited until she made a mistake of some kind, then he let her go.

After *The Young Lions*, for example, he got himself into a bad situation for a while. Back in New York again, he was living, following Movita's departure, with a French actress in the Carnegie apartment. It was a troubled relationship; they were always fighting. I came up to the apartment one

[134]

night just after they had been having a fearful argument, but Marlon was quite calm about it. There was only thing on his mind.

When she stormed out, he hurried to her jewel box, where she kept her diaphragm, to see if it was there. He knew how she operated. If she was really mad at him, it would be there and he knew she didn't want to be screwed. If it was gone, quarrel or not, he would know she was expecting sex. He was simply checking to see whether he was going to be laid that night. Meanwhile, he would wait to express his own anger. When she made a mistake—and she did—she would be gone, with her diaphragm.

As for me, matters were approaching a climax of some kind. I was still on junk, but Marlon was looking at me with new eyes after our work together on *Waterfront*. He was seeing me in a different light. On the set, I had always been beside him, and he had asked me a lot of questions about scenes. "How do you think that scene should go, Freddie?" he'd inquire. From the answers I gave him, he realized by the end of the picture that I could be of help to him.

Consequently, when Marlon left to go to the coast and do *Desirée*, he told me, "Try to kick the habit while I'm gone, and I think I can use you. When I get back, I'll find a job for you to do."

After he left, I went to work as a waiter at a place called the Montmartre, on West Fourth Street, in the Village. It was a restaurant and night club, owned by the son of an important Mafia figure, whom I happened to know. The headwaiter asked me if I would like to be a waiter there.

I liked the Montmartre. It was a jazz place, which drew a crowd of patrons that included a lot of well-known, and some less well-known, artists, writers, and poets, among others.

Charlie Parker, the great alto man, used to drop in and play for nothing. Other jazz musicians, like Stan Getz, and Larry Rivers, who later became a well-known painter, came by, and on good nights there were would be a regular line of musicians waiting to get on the stand and play together in this place, which had the kind of ambiance they liked. It was an "in" place, full of high-fashion models and their uptown friends, who mingled with the resident intellectuals. The help was mostly on junk, including me.

Marcia was often among the patrons, with the stylish friends she had made in her new job. We had broken up, in the way I've described, and I was living on Bank Street. I had been using pills to stave off the junk, but I was getting hooked again anyway. I was beginning to see that if I stayed in New York, I'd never get off the stuff.

New Year's Eve came and I had no place to go. After work, I called Marcia to wish her a happy New Year. It was about 2:30 in the morning, but I could hear party noises still going on when she picked up the phone, and I knew she must be celebrating in our old apartment, which she had made into a very elegant place after I left.

"What's going on?" I asked her after we had exchanged the usual greetings.

"Oh, we're just having a little party," she said.

"Who's there?"

She named all my old friends—jazz musicians, artists, people we'd known and that I'd known before we lived together. One of them was Allen Eager, who had been a friend for years.

"Put Allen on," I asked Marcia. "I'd like to wish him a happy New Year."

I could hear her calling him, but after a minute or two she came back and said, "He's in the middle of something and can't come to the phone just now."

*Marlon as Napoleon and Jean Simmons in the title role
of* Desirée. (TWENTIETH CENTURY-FOX)

I asked her to put some of the others I knew on the line,
but somehow it seemed that nobody could come to the phone
just then. I still didn't get the message.

"Well, it sounds as though you're having fun," I said. "Is it
all right to drop by and see you all?"

"No," Marcia said quickly, "it wouldn't be any use. The party's just breaking up."

Then I got it. For the first time, I realized I had alienated all my old friends. I not only hadn't been told about the party and was uninvited, but my old friends didn't really want to see me on New Year's Eve, or maybe any other time. Nobody wanted to have anything more to do with the junkie.

I knew it was time to get out. The last word I'd had from Marlon was an invitation. "If you stop using drugs and come out to Hollywood," he had written me, "I'll put you on as my stand-in for *Guys and Dolls*."

I decided to accept both the challenge and the invitation.

CHAPTER ELEVEN

I KICKED MY HABIT while I was traveling on a Greyhound bus from New York to Hollywood. The trip took five days and six nights, and knowing this, I had the sense to bring a fix with me, just in case. I didn't want to flip out during an acute attack of withdrawal symptoms and be thrown off the bus in the middle of nowhere. But the first four days of kicking are the worst. When I got over the hump, I threw away the fix, my "works," and everything else. This time I was really going to kick—and for the first time in years, I knew I wasn't kidding myself.

The bus arrived in Hollywood at last, and there I was in Dreamland, sick, seedy, and broke. Naturally, my first act was to look up Marlon. He was glad to see me, but he told me with a straight face that he was sorry, he'd forgotten that he had given his word to another guy, a Filipino-Mexican, a reformed pickpocket and petty thief who wanted to go legit. He was going to be the stand-in.

My look of absolute dismay brought a slight, sadistic smile to Marlon's lips, and after watching me stew in my disappointment for a moment, he beamed like a corny practical joker after a successful prank and told me that the part about the other guy was true but he had better plans for me. I was to be an "extra" with "call backs" that were guaranteed. When scenes didn't require extras, I would work as a "utility stand-in," which meant that I would stand-in for several actors. I'd be working every day, even when Marlon wasn't working, and I'd make more money that way.

So far, so good. The next job was to find a place to live. For the first few nights, I slept on a couch in the pad of a guy I knew, but then I ran into someone I'd known in New York, a girl named Mickey, a stunning Las Vegas blonde type. I told her my urgent need for a place to live, and she said, "I think I know someone who can put you up. I'll call her and see if we can't come for a swim this afternoon, and we'll see what happens."

The friend turned out to be Barbara Payton, who was recovering, if that is the word, from one of the biggest scandals Hollywood had seen in years. For those with short memories, Barbara had been married to Franchot Tone, but she had met Tom Neal, an actor who was a really tough muscleman, and they began to have an affair. Tone put detectives on her trail, and what they discovered put Tone in a rage and the whole story in the headlines. Particularly fascinating was the picture the enterprising detectives had managed to snap of Barbara dressed in the costume she liked to wear when she entertained Neal, which consisted of a black garter belt and beads. In the picture she was dressed in this costume, while her friend performed what the unsophisticated legal profession calls an "unnatural act." The outraged husband, with a singular lack of restraint, had several prints made and distributed the picture in the places where he thought it would do the most good.

After the scandal had died down, and the marriage had disappeared in a blaze of publicity, Barbara had settled down, so to speak, in her beautiful Beverly Hills house. Mickey and I met her there. We went for a swim, then sat at poolside, talking.

"I understand you need a place to stay," Barbara said, inspecting me carefully. "Why don't you stay here a while and see how you like it? You can have this little house by the pool. It's actually quite a nice apartment inside, and you can have it for $40 a month."

I accepted at once and took up my residence beside the pool. It didn't take me long to discover that Barbara had a new lover, a black man who used to arrive on a motorcycle. Sometimes I'd wander over to the main house when he was there, and a couple of times I inadvertently saw my landlady sitting between the legs of her visitor, going down on him, engaging in more of the "unnatural act" she seemed to be hung up on. Barbara heard me trying to walk quietly by and twisted her neck a little to see who it was, never missing a stroke.

She gave me to understand that I could stand in for her lover, but I had no eyes for her. In fact, there was only one lapse from our status of simple friendship—or landlady and tenant—and that occurred early one morning, about 2:00 A.M., when she appeared in my apartment and suggested her specialty. Apparently she was interested only in oral sex. There

[141]

Marlon with his Oscar.

was something off-center about this girl—not sexually, but in some strange fashion she seemed to drive men insane. Maybe they just couldn't understand or keep up with her mostly compulsive behavior.

In any case, Barbara and Mickey between them made my debut in Hollywood a spectacular, instant success. I couldn't help thinking how lucky I was. Two weeks ago I had been broke and addicted in New York, cast off by my friends and uninvited to their New Year's party. Now I had a job, I was free from dope at last, and I was riding down Sunset Boulevard in Barbara Payton's red Cadillac with her and Mickey, two gorgeous-looking broads. What a transition! I couldn't help laughing out loud when I thought about it.

"What are you laughing at?" Barbara wanted to know. But I couldn't really tell her.

Marlon came to visit me at Barbara's during the three months I stayed there. It was during this period, too, that he got an Academy Award for *Waterfront*, an event Barbara and I watched on television in her house. It was a lovely time for me, living there, and I was sorry when Barbara's finances suddenly collapsed. She lost the house and everything else. I stayed with other friends in Beverly Hills and eventually wound up with a French hooker who had a very nice apartment, where I came to rest for a while.

On the set of *Guys and Dolls*, where I began to work with Marlon, I was something of a curiosity. Although I was only an extra, I was always in his company—lunching with him, playing chess between setups, or just horsing around, then driving off with him at the end of the day. The "dolls" flocked around me, trying to wangle an introduction to my friend.

Among many other encounters, I observed the first meeting between Marlon and Frank Sinatra. They were to play a scene together in "Mindy's," a musical-comedy mockup of the original Lindy's in New York. Marlon was on the set early and ready to go to work. Sinatra appeared a few minutes later, brisk, blue eyes flashing, people jumping out of his way as he walked in a straight line, acting as though he owned everything in sight and everybody was on his payroll.

Joe Mankiewicz, the director, introduced him to Marlon. They shook hands and smiled. I thought Sinatra's smile was strained and unfelt. It was the kind of smile a professional fighter gives his opponent at the pre-fight weigh-in, but Marlon's was warm and genuine. Anyone could see that he was honestly delighted to meet the fabulous Sinatra.

Marlon likes to ease into a scene, to roam about on the set and absorb the atmosphere. He wants to glance at the extras, give a nod and smile to a familiar face. Sinatra, however, seemed impatient to get started; the movie was only one of many important things he had to do that day. Business associates were waiting in his dressing room. There were calls to make to Las Vegas, New York, and Florida. His entourage was gathered outside his dressing-room door, waiting to laugh at his jokes, light his cigarettes, hand him a drink, or bring him a hot dog—do anything for him, *anything*.

After a rehearsal or two, Marlon, Sinatra, and Mankiewicz decided to go for a take. Sinatra is a "one-or-two-take man," as they say in Hollywood, and he soon began to be exasperated because Marlon required many takes before he was satisfied with a scene. After eight or more out-takes, Sinatra, who was obliged to eat cheesecake during Marlon's dialogue, slammed his fork on the table, sprang to his feet, and yelled at Mankiewicz, "These fucking New York actors! How much cheesecake do you think I can eat?" And he walked off the set. Mankiewicz called for a five-minute break to ease the tension.

I thought Sinatra had overreacted, to put it as kindly as

*Frank Sinatra, Vivian Blaine, Jean Simmons, Marlon,
and Regis Toomey in* Guys and Dolls, *the only film
in which Marlon revealed his singing voice.*

possible, but his outburst seemed contrived, as though it had
been a deliberate attempt to embarrass Marlon.

Later, I learned that Marlon had snatched the Sky Masterson role (the romantic lead) right out of Sinatra's grasp. The
part was a natural for the singer. Sky Masterson was a con
man, a gambler, and a ladies' man. Knowing he could play
that kind of role to the hilt, Sinatra wanted it badly, but
Marlon came along, coveted it, and got it. Sinatra was offered the secondary role of Nathan Detroit, a small-time gambler who spoke with a thick Bronx-Jewish accent, and, to
everybody's surprise, he accepted it.

About a year before that, Sinatra had signed, or was very near to signing, a contract with Sam Spiegel to play Terry Malloy in *On the Waterfront*. Marlon had refused that role several times and then for some reason changed his mind and took it. Sinatra was dropped. To compound his humiliation, while *Guys and Dolls* was being filmed, Marlon won an oscar for his portrayal of Terry Malloy in *Waterfront*.

It was no secret in Hollywood that Sinatra carried grudges for a long, long time, and one of his cronies told me that he was determined to "sing Marlon right off the screen." Both Marlon and I were on hand, along with many other spectators, who gathered around to see him try to do that when he played his first musical scene. (For the uninitiated, I should explain that the musical sequences are previously recorded in a soundproof studio, then played back while the actors mouth the lyrics and synchronize their movements to the sound.)

Sinatra came on the set dressed as Nathan Detroit, the lowbrow character with a thick accent who had been played on the Broadway stage by Sam Levene, an actor who specializes in Bronx-Jewish characters. Levene spoke and *sang* in character, which is the way it must be if the character is to remain consistent. In the film, Sinatra delivered his lines with only the faintest suggestion of an accent, but in character. When he sang, however, he sang as himself—smooth, lyrical, romantic. And out of character.

I was standing behind Marlon, peering at the scene over his shoulder, and he slowly turned around until we were standing face to face. He was a little pale and whispered harshly, "He's playing *my* part. *He's* not the romantic lead. *I* am."

Marlon went over to Mankiewicz, who was standing nearby, and said, "Joe, Frank's playing his part all wrong. He's supposed to sing with a Bronx accent. He's supposed to

[146]

clown it up. But he's singing like a romantic lead. We can't have *two* romantic leads."

"I agree with you," Mankiewicz said. "What do you suggest I do about it?"

"Tell him!" Marlon said. "Tell him!"

The notion of "telling" Sinatra how he should sing a song brought a wry smile to Joe's lips. "*You* tell him," he said and walked away.

Marlon was dumbstruck for a few seconds. When he recovered, he said, "It's not *my* job to tell him. It's the director's job. I'm never going to work with Mankiewicz again."

The filming went on without incident. But except for the formal exchange of greetings in passing, Marlon and Frank never spoke to each other. Two separate camps were formed at opposite ends of the vast set. Marlon's crowd was at one end, Sinatra's at the other, and they never mingled. Since then, their paths have not crossed. I don't imagine much effort has been made on either side.

One day Marlon and I were talking on the set, when I saw that he was looking at something over my shoulder.

"Don't turn around now," he said, "but there's an extra with black hair, red dress, and red shoes. Wait . . . wait . . . you can look now, but be discreet."

I turned, saw the girl he meant, and I did a double-take. Girl? She was easily fifty-five, her black hair was blatantly dyed, her large breasts were sagging so that they fell nearly to her navel, and her legs were so thin in proportion to the bulk above that she seemed top-heavy.

"Man, are you kidding?" I said. "You must be even more nearsighted than I thought you were. That broad is *old*, and she's ugly as sin."

"You fuck your women, and I'll fuck mine," Marlon said calmly. "Try to get her number for me," he added.

[147]

Marlon and Jean Simmons in Guys and Dolls.

I approached the lady and told her that Marlon would like to call her after the day's work. Nearly overcome, she gave me her number, and I returned with it.

"How'd you get it so quick?" Marlon asked seriously. "How do you do it?"

Since I had just done what must have been the easiest thing anyone could imagine, I was sure he was putting me on.

"It's my irresistible charm," I said sarcastically.

I tried to find out next day if he had really followed up, but he wouldn't talk about it. I could only conclude that on occasion he must be as freakish as I was.

It wasn't often I was able to put *him* on, but I did it successfully while we were finishing *Guys and Dolls* in Hollywood. He was coming out frequently to see me at the French hooker's house, where I was living, and if I didn't see him for a day or two, he would call me. It was plain that he depended on my being there when he needed me, and that gave me the idea for the put-on.

I was always supposed to call him if I didn't hear from him, so one day he was on the telephone saying accusingly, "You haven't called me."

"I'm leaving town tomorrow," I told him.

"*What?*" he yelled. "You aren't going back to New York and get on that shit again?"

"I've gotta leave this town," I said. "Something's happened, Marlon. I went into a bar yesterday and picked up this lovely chick. She was wearing a sweater with long sleeves, and I could see she had nice tits. We had a drink and decided we were going to ball. We went to her place, but when we got there, she told me she was having her period, but she'd go down on me. She said she wouldn't take off her clothes, though. So I said okay, and we were just about to do it when two dicks from the vice squad busted in. They'd been following us, apparently. But then was the big surprise, Marlon. You wouldn't believe it. This girl with the nice tits turns out to be a man, a transvestite, so I'm picked up on a homosexual rap. How do you like that?"

Marlon said anxiously, "Did you know it was a boy?"

"No, I was completely fooled."

"Well, don't use my name now, but I'll get you a smart lawyer and there won't be any trouble. I'll get you out of this."

I couldn't carry it on any further and broke up.

Marlon laughed too. "You put me on, you bastard," he said, but he sounded amused. In fact, he loved to be put on, except when the put-on failed, and then he could be quite irritated.

CHAPTER TWELVE

AFTER *Guys and Dolls* was finished, Paramount wanted Marlon to make a Western, and they did an astounding thing for a studio. They offered him full control of the film, final cut and all. It was a rare opportunity, and Marlon took them up on it immediately. At the same time, he formed his own company, giving it his mother's maiden name, Pennebaker Productions. He put George Glass and Walter Selzer at the head, and they promptly produced three bombs: *Shake Hands with the Devil, Last Train from Madrid,* and *Paris Blues.*

By this time, Marlon's activities were so numerous that he had to take on more help, and one of the help he took on was his father. Dodie had died the year before, and Senior was alone. Dodie's passing had been very difficult for everybody. While she was lying ill, Marlon asked me to write her a letter. I did the best I could, hardly knowing what to say to someone in that position, especially someone I loved, like Dodie. It was the hardest letter to compose that I've ever written. I wrote that I loved her, that I missed her, and urged her to get well soon because I was aching to see her again. Later, I found out that my letter had arrived too late. Marlon went to Libertyville, of course, and was with her when she died. He sent me a long, touching, laboriously written letter, which I still have, describing her death. She died, he wrote, with dignity and great style.

When Marlon came back to Hollywood, looking very gloomy, he said nothing more about Dodie. I respected his deep hurt and said nothing either. But he did ask me to write a letter to his father, which I did. I told him I realized how he must be feeling, to lose such a wonderful woman after so many years of marriage, but I was sure it must be gratifying to have lived with such an extraordinary person. Senior never answered the letter and didn't even mention it when we met again in Hollywood.

After Dodie's death, Senior went rapidly downhill. His investments failed one by one until there were none left. These included a cattle-raising venture in Nebraska, into which Marlon had put a considerable amount of his own money. That went with the rest. Senior had always led Marlon to believe that he was an astute businessman, but now it was apparent that he never had been; it was all façade. It was clear that he had never been much more than a traveling salesman and not a very good one at that.

Now he was alone and broke, and Marlon gave him a job, nominally as treasurer of Pennebaker Productions, but actu-

Two Marlon Brandos, Senior and Junior.
(WARNER BROS. PICTURES INC.)

ally he was only a paper shuffler, doing minor chores in the office. He still looked like a solid, prosperous, Midwestern businessman, but it was clear that even this appearance wouldn't last long either. He was a sad man, his wife gone, forced to accept a job in a world he despised, in effect taking charity from his son and too old to go on the road any more.

Marlon was respectful enough to him, but they rarely saw each other, and one day there was a scene between them, when I was present, that was dramatic evidence of the ironic reversal of roles between father and son.

I was in Marlon's office at Paramount, discussing something about a script. Marlon had leaned back in his swivel chair, removing his shoes and resting his heels on the desk. He summoned his father on the intercom, and presently Senior entered. Marlon didn't ask his father to sit down, nor did he stand up to greet him. I wanted to be excused, but he insisted I stay.

"Is the check ready for me to sign?" Marlon asked.

It was a check for $5,000 which he had asked to be drawn for Stella Adler. She had produced a revival of *He Who Gets Slapped* on Broadway, which had been given some good reviews, but more capital was needed to keep it running while word of mouth, which she was certain would happen, generated the steam to assure it of a run. Marlon knew there wasn't much hope, but he had no hesitation in giving her the money when she asked. He was immensely grateful to the Adler family for the help and encouragement they had given him at the beginning of his own career.

But in answer to Marlon's question, Senior said, "No."

"Why not?" Marlon inquired, raising an eyebrow.

"There isn't enough cash to cover a check of that size."

"What! Are you saying I haven't got five thousand bucks?"

"Not in cash. You'll have to liquidate some of your assets.

Selling bonds before they mature isn't a very good idea. You lose a lot of money that way. And from what I hear, if you invest in the play, you'll lose the whole five thousand."

"I'm not *investing* in a *play*," Marlon said in exasperation. "I'm *lending* money to a *friend*, an old friend who needs it."

"I know. But I hear she's going to use the money to keep a failing play running. It's throwing good money after bad."

"I don't care what she does with the money. This is a personal loan, not a business deal."

"Five thousand dollars in hard cash is a lot of money. When you consider how much you have to earn in order to keep five—"

"Make out a check for five thousand," Marlon snapped, "and bring it here for me to sign."

Senior blushed and turned to leave, but Marlon stopped him. "From now on," he said, "when I tell you that I want to lend money to a friend, I don't want to hear about assets and taxes and all that. Just do as I say."

Senior left quietly and closed the door carefully behind him.

Marlon turned to me and said, "Jesus, I hate to order people around like that. But what can I do?"

"He's not people," I said. "He's your father."

"I know. And that makes it worse. I guess he means well. He wants to show me that he's keeping a sharp eye on my money, but he's trying too hard. I wish he'd relax."

It was much too late for Senior to relax. Marlon had gotten him to go to a shrink, citing how much help analysis had been to him ever since *Streetcar*, when he had begun it himself. Senior went reluctantly and soon quit, maybe because he was chintzy about money even when it was Marlon's. He remarried, a woman who looked very much like Dodie, much younger and also an alcoholic. It was not a happy marriage.

I didn't share Marlon's early confidence that analysis might help his father, because I couldn't see that it had done much for Marlon, although he was on the couch on a more or less regular schedule except when he was on location. As he grew more successful, I could see him changing in some ways. At the beginning he had been deeply loyal to his friends, and God knows he had done enough for me, but now there was less and less evidence of his early loyalty and self-sacrificing characteristics. He was putting limits on his generosity, becoming more and more absorbed in himself.

One thing that concerned him was the image he presented to the public. We got to talking about it one morning, in a roundabout way, over breakfast. I hadn't meant to be there for breakfast at all, having driven over the previous afternoon in my '41 Ford convertible, which I called a car only out of courtesy. I couldn't get the top up, the windshield wiper didn't work, and it was always full of leaves and other debris from the trees, under whose branches it stood every night unprotected. It was such an absolute wreck that I had to ask the host or hostess in advance when I was invited to a party if there were any steep hills in the neighborhood that the car might not be able to climb. I always had to park it downhill to get it started.

That was the vehicle I drove to Marlon's house, so ashamed of it that I parked it around the bend of the road, out of sight, and walked the rest of the way. We spent the afternoon and evening as we so often did, talking about a thousand things, eating, just fooling around, and when I got up to go, Marlon said, "Why don't you stay over tonight?" I agreed.

Next morning, while we were getting breakfast, he got to talking about images and how hard it was to change them. People still thought he was Stanley Kowalski, he complained, whenever they met him. "I can't get rid of that Kowalski image," Marlon said. "You know I'm the exact opposite of his type, Freddie. Everybody who knows me knows I'm a gentleman."

As he talked, he was putting Ry-Krisp crackers in the toaster, preparing one of his favorite breakfasts. When they popped up, he sloshed some butter on them and picked one up, but it was too hot to handle as he tried to eat it. The melted butter ran down the sides of his face, and as he tried desperately to save it, throwing his head back, it began to run into his ears as he grabbed for a napkin. He was a mess.

"I don't know why this image of you persists when you've got so much style and class," I told him seriously.

Seeing him wipe off the butter reminded me of another time when, after screwing a girl and having an orgasm, he went down on her and the semen trickled back into his ears, like the butter. But Stanley Kowalski he wasn't. He was right about that.

If there was one thing about Marlon that didn't change, it was his single-mindedness about trying to fuck every broad in the world, particularly if she happened to be my girl first. A striking example was the case of an exotic-looking East Indian, always the kind he liked.

This episode came about through my friendship with Tony, a chorus girl in Billy Rose's Diamond Horseshoe, a long since extinct New York night club. For a time Tony had been Marlon's mistress, to use an old and inadequate word. She was tall, brunette, and statuesque in the traditional Ziegfeld mold, and she had a great ass, which was always Marlon's primary criterion for feminine beauty.

Through Tony I met her friend Elizabeth, and I was struck at once by her beauty. She was slim, completely charming, and her lovely skin was as dark and smooth as stained mahogany that has been rubbed to a fine luster. Elizabeth worked for Air India as a travelers' aide. Her voice had the boarding-school English accent that characterizes girls who have gone to good Indian schools, just as it does in England.

The day I met her, she and Tony picked me up in Tony's car and we drove around town, stopping here and there to talk, eat, drink, and listen to jazz. Elizabeth and I hit it off immediately, so intensely attracted to each other that when Tony left her alone with me later at my apartment, we fell right into bed and screwed all night.

As time went on, she seemed to be genuinely in love with me, buying me little gifts, according to Indian custom, like a turtleneck sweater and a set of handkerchiefs. When I saw how serious she was getting about me, I tried to cool it because I had no intention of getting that much involved with her or any other girl. I made excuses for not seeing her, and when she told me that she had begun seeing Marlon, presumably to make me jealous, I was relieved rather than annoyed.

I hadn't seen her for a week or two when the phone rang one evening about eight o'clock, and it was Marlon. He came right on without any preliminary:

"Hello, Freddie. Have you been to bed with Elizabeth?"

"I don't think it's any of your fucking business," I said.

"Yes it is, Freddie."

"Why is it?"

"Because I'm going with her, and we're about to be engaged."

"Well, congratulations," I said, and meant it.

"Thanks, but have you ever been to bed with her?"

"I still think it's none of your business."

"I'm having dinner with her right now in that Mexican restaurant we go to."

"Did she tell you I had?"

"No."

"Then what makes you think I did?"

"Well, I told her I had a friend who liked fat girls, and I told her about the one you wanted to fuck so badly, you know, the one who weighed about two hundred pounds, and you were ashamed to be seen going around with her." I could have added that she was also young and voluptuous and no meatball.

"So I was telling her about my friend who sometimes just had to have a fat broad," Marlon went on, "and how there just wasn't any way you could hide this one. She thought that was pretty funny, and naturally she wanted to know my friend's name."

"What did you say?"

"I told her. She turned absolutely white, Freddie, and you know how hard that would be for her, so when I saw that, I knew she must have gone to bed with you. That's why I'm calling you, Freddie. Did you?"

"Look, man, what's the difference? Isn't anybody else allowed to screw your girls? And anyway, even if you didn't permit it, how was I supposed to know that when she hadn't even met you?"

I knew he wanted me to say, for those strange, interior reasons of his own that came up so often in his relations with women, that I had fucked Liz—and say it straight out, a plain statement, or, more like it, a confession.

"I know what you want me to say," I told him, "and I know why you want me to say it. So you can go back to the table and tear her head off."

Marlon didn't pursue it. "Okay, Freddie," he said, and went back to his dinner.

She finally confessed, I found out later, that she had been

Marlon and the author discussing a woman.

screwing me, and at that point she hadn't yet been to bed with Marlon, although I have no doubt she began to do so that night.

"What were you so excited about?" I asked Marlon when I saw him again. "You're not only jealous of me when I'm fucking girls you've made it with, but even of the ones I've been to bed with *before* you have."

He wouldn't explain, just passed it off. His affair with Elizabeth went on for another month or so, but she was a different kind of girl from any he'd had before. For one thing, she was sensible and had no ambition to be a movie star, or to advance a professional career, like so many of the ones who had affairs with Marlon. She didn't give a damn about Hollywood glamour, and as far as she was concerned, what she wanted from Marlon was not any of the things that went with his name, but simply a home and a man she could love. To understate it, Marlon was not a homemaker, so although I believe he really cared for her in his way, nothing could come of it, and when she realized that, the affair ended. Later she married an English architect, and as far as I know it was a happy marriage.

Elizabeth may have been a warm-up, so to speak, for a much more important relationship in Marlon's life, his affair and eventual marriage with Anna Kashfi. So much has been written about that relationship, a great deal of it ugly, that it's hard to believe now it started the way it did.

Marlon told me one day that he had met an Indian girl. He seemed to be most impressed by the fact that she was a virgin. Shortly after, she went into the City of Hope Hospital because it was suspected that she might have tuberculosis. Marlon asked me to go over there and meet her one day; apparently, he had already made several visits. He was going to take a projector with him, he said, and some film and try to cheer her up a little. That night, and later, he ran a whole film festival for her, particularly *Singing in the Rain,* one of his favorite movies.

When I first saw Anna, I was as charmed as Marlon had been. She was a tall, slim girl with large, dark eyes and a seeming sweetness about her that fooled me completely. Obviously, she was much attracted to Marlon and almost pathetically grateful for all the attention he was showing her.

After a few of these meetings, Marlon asked me pointblank, "Well, what do you think of her?"

"She's the best you've had so far," I said. "Very sweet. Lots of class."

"I'm thinking of marrying her."

"Well, I think she'd make you a great wife. But I hope

[160]

you're really in love with her. If you love her enough to marry her, then—I think it's great."

They didn't get married right away, and I would have thought that might have given Marlon enough time to see the tigress slowly emerging from his sweet and charming virgin, but if he saw, he didn't immediately draw back, as I'd seen him do before when a girl gave him any trouble.

He had two commitments to fulfill before he could begin work on the Western that Paramount had offered him carte blanche to produce. One was *Sayonara*, for William Goetz, and the other was *The Young Lions*, the second half of his settlement promise to Zanuck.

Josh Logan was to direct *Sayonara*, and Marlon had some doubts about him, but they vanished when, during a conference, he saw the tender care and delicacy Logan employed to pick the dead, dry leaves from an ivy plant on the windowsill. That was the kind of attention the picture needed, Marlon thought.

While the *Sayonara* preparations were going on, I didn't see him for a while, or at least no more than once or twice a week, and I thought it was a little peculiar. But I had my own car by this time, and my own friends, so I didn't think too much of it. Occasionally Marlon would call me up and ask me if I could get a girl for some friend of his from out of town. My friend the French hooker was always happy to oblige. She was not actually in the business of running a house, but she did have a lot of willing friends, and if the occasion called for it, she was ready to offer herself, if not to a visiting fireman, then to someone like the retired Metropolitan Opera soprano who lived not far away.

I heard that Marlon had a new friend, a screen writer named George Englund, whom he seemed to be as close to as he had always been with me, and I thought maybe that was why I hadn't been seeing him. Marlon had been paying him out of his own funds, and when George made the mistake of asking him for a raise, Brando was disenchanted and fired him.

Not long after, Marlon said to me abruptly, "How'd you like to work for me?"

"Okay," I said.

"Good. I'll give you two hundred and fifty dollars a week and an expense account. Okay?"

"Okay, it's a deal, for two hundred and fifty and a pencil."

"Fine. You can begin right now. I want you to read the *Sayonara* script and tell me what you think of it."

I did, and it was absolutely terrible, women's-magazine shit. Poor Josh Logan, I thought. If he can make anything out of this, he's a genius.

While I was reading it, Marlon made me another of his quick propositions: "How'd you like to come to Japan as my dialogue coach?"

"Ah'd like dat jus' fine," I said, doing my Uncle Tom shuffling bit that always broke him up.

"Have you got a passport?"

"Nope. But I'll get one."

"Do that right away. We've got a couple of weeks before shooting, and I want to use that time to start working on the script for the Western."

"Are you going to write it too?"

"Yeah. Why not? I've read so many lousy scripts, I thought I'd try one myself. We'll go to Honolulu and bounce some ideas around."

"Writing ain't all that easy, chum," I said. "Think you can do better than the old pros?"

"Old *hacks*, you mean," Marlon said. "I could piss a better script in the snow."

I finished reading the *Sayonara* script, and now I had something of a dilemma. If I told Marlon how awful I thought it was, I might blow both the trip to Japan and my new job. I thought about it and decided I had to tell him the truth, no matter what.

"Don't do this picture," I told him. "This script is one of the worst I've ever read. It's way beneath your talent."

"It's too late," Marlon said. "I've already signed to do it. We can't even think about *not* doing it. And anyway, I need the loot. We'll just have to punch up the script, maybe play down the love story and play up the social stuff. But I'm glad you told me the truth, Freddie."

I was glad too. I realized that if I had told him it was great, he'd know that either I was lying or I had no judgment, because he knew as well as I did how bad it was. If I had lied, I never would have gotten to Japan.

As the time approached to go, Marlon surveyed me critically one day. I was dressed in my usual casual disarray, the result of not having any money to speak of, and habitual indifference, which I suppose was part of my junkie past. At the moment I was tastefully gotten up in sneakers and an old pair of slacks. Until then I had only one criterion where clothes were concerned: If you can't throw it in the water and get it clean, don't wear it.

"You've got to get yourself some clothes, man, before we go to see those Japanese broads," Marlon said. "I'll open up an account for you at Carroll and Company."

That was the best men's store in Hollywood, and I found myself there next day, where I'd never expected to be, buying myself a dark-blue blazer, gray slacks, and some shoes. Then I showed my new wardrobe proudly to Marlon.

"Is this all you bought?" he asked incredulously. "You can't get around on that, man. Go back and get yourself some more clothes."

So I went back and splurged—a suit, more shoes, a sports jacket, slacks, something for every occasion. I'd never had such a wardrobe in my life. I was looking good, then, when I got the surprise of my life. The phone rang and it was Marcia; she had just flown in from New York. Somehow, through mutual friends, she had heard I was doing well with Marlon and was about to go to Japan. She came directly from the airport to the small apartment I had on Honey Drive, in a building that had once been a whorehouse and gambling joint.

When I opened the door, we fell into each other's arms, as though nothing had ever happened. Suddenly I was more in love with her than ever, and apparently she still was, too. We fucked all night long and had a complete reconciliation.

"Don't go away again," I said next morning. "Come and live with me."

"I can't do that. You know my folks live right here in Los Angeles, and I want to see them too. If we're going to live together, we'll have to get married."

"Wonderful," I said. "We'll do it just as soon as I get back from Japan."

A couple of nights later we went out to dinner with Marlon and Anna Kashfi. Marcia hadn't changed her mind about Marlon; she still couldn't stand him. But she and Anna took one look and instantly adored each other. They were soon talking so animatedly that they scarcely noticed Marlon and me. It was an immediate and lasting friendship.

That was something for them to develop. Meanwhile, Marlon and I were going to Japan.

CHAPTER THIRTEEN

W

E WENT TO Honolulu
first. Traveling with a superstar is an experience that boggles
the mind. Chauffeured limousines are always at hand to pick
you up and drop you at hotels, airports—wherever. After you
have packed your luggage, it is carried off and reappears safe
and sound in another country, in your hotel suite, a suite you
didn't even bother to register for. The Music Corporation of
America, Marlon's agent at the time, made all the arrangements, and it was as good as having your own genie. The most
ordinary incidents—taking the elevator, for instance—became
great fun. I was always amused when the elevator doors opened,

[165]

and the passengers' faces lighted up as Marlon entered and stood among them in such awful proximity.

Marlon was overweight and had to slim down in order to fit into his costumes. He couldn't bear the sight of seeing me stuff myself with the marvelous food we were having in Honolulu, and although I was slim, he persuaded me to diet with him—for company. Marlon also thought he needed exercise, knowing well enough that I hate exercise, so I was obliged to trot beside him as he jogged great distances along the Honolulu beach. He loved to toss a football as high and far as he could. I was elected to run and catch it. I'm a lousy receiver, and once, as I turned to chase a particularly high, long toss, the football plummeted down from the sky and hit me on the head. It felt as though I had been struck by a meteorite, and I quit the game on the spot. As soon as my brains stopped rattling around, Marlon had me footracing on the hard, wet sand.

We invented a kind of crazy weight-reducing diet—only vegetables, all kinds of low-calorie vegetables, to be eaten raw or parboiled. Nothing must be added to them, we ruled. No butter, no salt or pepper, no sauces, no nothing. He made me take an oath that this was all we would eat until he had lost sixteen pounds. No cheating. It never occurred to him that *I* might also lose sixteen pounds, and that much off my slim frame would make me look as emaciated as the victim of a famine.

After four or five days of that dreary vegetable diet, we fell into long silences, unable to think about anything but steak, lobster, pork chops, broiled fish—thoughts that Marlon, with his passion for junk food, would never ordinarily have entertained at all. Over impossibly long distances we could smell a hamburger cooking on a grill. Each of us wished the other would weaken and break the other. But we were caught up in a contest of will power. Who would weaken first? I had

[166]

been a drug addict, but Marlon was a food addict, never mind that his palate was anything but discriminating. My victory was only a question of time.

One morning I awoke earlier than usual, snapping quickly to consciousness as though someone had turned me on, and I felt immediately that something was wrong. Maybe it was only hunger. In any case, I decided to check up on Marlon. I went to the balcony and climbed over the divider which separated our adjoining terraces. I peered into his bedroom. The bed had been slept in, but it was empty. I knew instinctively where he was and ran out of the hotel.

I found him at the corner drugstore, gorging himself. He had already emptied a pint-sized glass of fresh orange juice, and he was polishing off a large bowl of cornflakes with sliced bananas and cream, as the waitress was appearing with plates of scrambled eggs, sausages, and bacon, and a high deck of pancakes dripping with melted butter.

"What the hell are you doing?" I asked, a little redundantly. "Are you nuts? If you finish this breakfast, you'll look like Charles Laughton."

I grabbed his arm and tried to pull him away from the counter. He pushed me away and growled. I might as well have tried to pull away a hungry lion from his kill. I had come away in such a hurry that I was dressed in a minimum of clothing, sockless in unlaced sneakers, my uncombed hair standing on end. The customers must have thought I was a lunatic, and a couple of beefy guys at the counter looked at me threateningly.

I got panicky and announced to the customers, "He's supposed to be on a diet for a movie. And it's my job to see he stays on it."

"Sit down," Marlon whispered fiercely. "You're making a jackass of yourself."

I sat beside him and watched him pour half a jug of maple syrup over his butter-soaked pancakes.

"Why don't *you* have something?" Marlon said. Before I could answer, he signaled the waitress and asked her to duplicate the order for me. Taking solemn oaths to resume our diets tomorrow, we stuffed ourselves to the tonsils, without guilt.

After breakfast, we went back to our Hawaiian-style cottage to work. We were already mulling around with the Western for Paramount, a project that was beginning to absorb more and more of Marlon's thoughts. He told me he didn't want to make the old, classic Western. He wanted to scramble good and evil in the characters of the "good guys" and "bad guys," put the hero on the black horse, the villain on the white one, and all that.

On that premise, we began improvising scenes. Marlon would record them on tape, and I would have them typewritten by a public stenographer. Now and then he'd insert a crazy phrase—"and Rio removes his wooden, hand-carved dental plates, puts them in his pocket, and kisses and gums the heroine on her left tit"—just to test the stenographer, to see whether she was a mere mechanic or whether she was interested enough to read the manuscript. He was delighted to see, after one such insane sentence, the stenographer's notation, "Well, really!" and "Are you serious?"

Marlon had decided to call the Western *A Burst of Vermilion*. It was a fancy title, born of an inspiration so childish that Hopalong Cassidy would have cringed in embarrassment. It was Marlon's idea to have his gang of bank robbers and murderers tie blood-red scarves around their necks that would snap in the wind as they galloped on the purple sage toward some nefarious adventure. *A Burst of Vermilion*—get it?

I was a little bewildered when he told me. I wondered why

the outlaws would herald their intent to murder and plunder by wearing red scarves. Wouldn't they rather try to pass themselves off as ordinary, honest cowpokes who were only passing through?

Marlon cast his eyes toward the ceiling and thought about it. No, he said at last, the red scarves would work cinematically. In the beginning, the capers were not to be treated seriously, but lightly, like kids playing a game. The outlaws chose their way of life for the excitement of it, rather than for the money. In fact, money meant very little to them. As soon as they got their hands on a bundle, they squandered it as quickly as they could, on women, booze, and gambling. The outlaws were nonentities looking for an identity, even as thieves. The red scarves were symbolic of all this, Marlon said.

I thought my dear friend was losing his mind, but prudently I held my tongue. I knew he'd come to his senses later and delete the red-scarf business. And he did. I've noticed that when genius lapses, sometimes it slips into idiocy.

Our rooms in the Honolulu hotel were adjoining, but not in the American sense. They were separated by sliding doors that met in the center, except that they were warped and couldn't be tightly closed. If I chose, I could look through directly to the bed and right up Marlon's ass while he was screwing some broad, which was quite a lot of the time. His most frequent companion was a Hawaiian dancer, who was a marvelous swimmer as well, but her best talents were in bed.

She had been displaying them most of one night when Marlon got a phone call early in the morning. Anna was at the airport. She had just flown in from Los Angeles and she was coming right over.

Marlon burst into my room. "Annie's here," he said.

"Well, so what?" I said.

"So *what*? We've got to go through this room with a fine-tooth comb and find every piece of female hair and bobby pin we can. If she finds the least little bit of evidence that I've had a girl up here, I won't hear the end of it."

Already, I could see, he was a little afraid of her. It was not a good sign.

For an hour we cleaned that room frantically, searching in every crevice, especially around the bed and in the bathroom. I don't think the hotel maid had ever given the place such a thorough cleaning. We had just finished when Anna appeared, all radiant smiles and love. Marlon didn't have time or opportunity for anyone else until it was time to go on to Japan.

When we landed in Tokyo, Josh Logan and several Japanese dignitaries greeted us with deep bows, toothy grins, and rapid, unintelligible English. We were whisked into long, black limousines and zipped through the horrendous traffic with sirens screaming. We were installed in separate suites at a hotel in the heart of Tokyo.

In the morning, Marlon was to start on a busy schedule of interviews, press conferences, diplomatic dinner parties, and so on and so forth. That evening, however, he would be free until nine o'clock, and it was only five in the evening. He was excited about being in Japan, and the tension had been building. He wanted to relax. And he was horny.

"Wanna get laid?" he asked me.

"Always," I said. "And all ways."

"Ever been to bed with a geisha?"

"Nope. I've never been with an Asian. I've heard geishas are great in bed."

"Who told you that?"

"A couple of guys who were here during the war."

[171]

"They probably meant the girls that hang around the bars. Americans call them geishas, but they're not—not really."

"What makes geishas so special?"

"Well, they're brought up since early childhood to entertain. And that's all they do—entertain. They're taught all the social graces. They sing, play an instrument, and they dance. They enact little scenes for you in pantomime. They sit beside you at dinner and see that your plate is never empty and make sure your sake cup is always filled. When the conversation breaks down, you can depend on them to come into the breach with some chatter. And if your joke falls flat, she'll laugh herself silly to spare you any embarrassment. After dinner, she'll give you a massage and a bath, then roll out the mattress and screw your ears off."

"I know a couple of hookers who'll do all that for you and more," I said.

"You've got no class, Freddie." Marlon sighed. "You're still a lowbrow from Brooklyn. Come on. If we're gonna go, we'd better get started. The guy who gave me the address told me it was on the other side of town. And we've got to be back by nine."

"It's only five. That gives us four hours."

"We've got less than that, when you consider traveling time and ceremonies."

"Ceremonies? What ceremonies?"

"I *told* you, man. These chicks have style. *Style.*"

In the street, we hailed a cab, and Marlon gave the driver a look at a slip of paper with an address written in Japanese. The cabbie bobbed his head vigorously. Yes, he knew the place.

We climbed in and the taxi took off like a shot. There is no traffic in the world—not in New York, Paris, Berlin, Rome, or Los Angeles—that is as jammed, swift, and scarily aggressive as the traffic in Tokyo. There were no speed limits, at least not then. Traffic lights were rare, placed far apart at great distances, and they went unheeded. Nobody yielded to anybody; somebody was always screeching to a stop. When they stepped into a car, the gentle Japanese were transformed into fierce Samurai warriors.

We drove in this heart-stopping fashion for fifteen minutes, then a half hour, then forty-five minutes, then an hour. The driver kept increasing his speed and he was getting wilder and wilder. Marlon and I exchanged wondering looks. We knew we should have arrived at our destination some thirty minutes ago.

"I think this guy's lost," I said.

"I think so too," Marlon agreed.

"Tell him to stop and let us out. We'll get another cab."

"We can't do that. That's an insult. You don't insult people in Japan. It just isn't done."

"Well, what *do* you do in Japan when you're in a situation like this?"

"Nothing. You just wait it out."

Suddenly the driver jammed on the brakes, double-parked, leaped out, leaving the door wide open, and ran into a grocery store, waving the slip of paper with the address written on it. Marlon and I watched him and the storekeeper consulting street maps, and after several minutes of scrutiny and much scratching of heads in perplexity, they found the place we were looking for. The driver ran back to the taxi, jumped in, and we were off again.

"He should have done that more than a half hour ago," I said.

"Patience," Marlon advised me.

"This crazy cabbie has shortened our time in bed with geishas by a half hour, at the least."

"If you're going to enjoy your stay in Japan, have patience," Marlon said, with the complacent look of a Buddhist philosopher. "Observe the Japanese and do as they do. They'd rather lose a half hour than hurt anyone's feelings with complaints."

After zigzagging another fifteen minutes on the main drag, we turned into a deserted alley so narrow it hardly allowed passage for the small taxi. At the end of it, we were confronted by a brick wall. We had come to a dead end, and our destination was nowhere in sight.

Marlon tried to contain himself, but I could see he had come to the end of his patience. He was ready to blow his stack. He shifted his weight from one buttock to the other, his ears flattened, and his eyes narrowed. The driver, now wilder than ever, put the car in reverse and backed out of the alley at breakneck speed. We backtracked onto the main street again, drove down a block and turned into another narrow alley. It was a serene, tree-lined, cobblestoned street, and we stopped before a small, lovely house with tiny fountains and yellow lamps glowing with halos in the mist.

The driver turned to us, reached over and opened the door, indicating that we had arrived.

"You stay in the cab while I check the place out," Marlon said to me. "This guy might be trying to dump us."

He got out, went to the door and knocked. Presently it opened and I saw Marlon smile and exchange a few words with somebody inside.

"Okay, you can cut him loose," Marlon called. "We're here."

I got out of the cab, paid the fare, and gave the driver a generous tip. He grinned, blew out his breath in relief that he hadn't lost face, and drove away. I joined Marlon, and we entered the house.

We found ourselves in one of the prettiest rooms I would

ever see in Japan. It was sparsely but exquisitely furnished. The polished hardwood floor was spread with tatami mats, and on the low tables of brilliant black lacquer were placed slim, graceful vases containing miniature roses. On the walls were scrolls of rice paper and silk, depicting surrealistic Japanese landscapes. In painted pots, I saw the amazing bonsai trees, dwarfed by special methods of culture—real, live trees that were tiny replicas of their giant brothers.

The shriveled, middle-aged woman who had let us in left us for a moment. She returned leading a petite, delicate girl of seventeen or so. She was dressed in the classical Japanese style. Her elaborate pile of lacquered hair was held in place with combs of tortoise shell, and her embroidered kimono swept the floor. Her skin was powdered clown white, and her natural eyebrows had been shaven off and replaced with painted brows arching high above her dark almond eyes. She walked with such small, mincing steps that I would have sworn her feet, hidden under the floor-length kimono and wrapped in binding, were no larger than an infant's. She was a living doll, as mechanical as a toy, as artificial as porcelain sculpture, an *objet d'art*.

"This one is mine," Marlon said in a raspy voice, turning to me.

"Where's mine?" I whispered back.

"The old lady is yours," he said. "You always said you liked older women."

"Come on. This is no time for jokes. Where's mine?"

Marlon spoke with the mama-san in a mixture of Japanese and pig Latin, and somehow she understood what he meant. She skittered across the room, went through an archway, then reappeared with someone who could have been the twin of the first girl. She introduced us all. We sat on silk pillows and were served spiced apples, strong bitter tea, and cookies that

[175]

tasted like burnt honey. As far as I could tell, the conversation was made up of compliments and the polite acknowledgment of compliments. After quite a while of this "happy talk," I began to wonder. When was my geisha going to lead me away to a private chamber and screw my ears off as Marlon had promised?

Marlon looked at his watch, said something in Japanese, and we all got to our feet. He took the mama-san aside for a private business talk, and soon they returned.

"Let's go," he said to me, "or I'll be late for my appointment."

"But what about—"

"Let's go," Marlon said sternly.

We said our good-byes, exchanging compliments as we went, and stepped out into the foggy night. We walked to the main drag, hailed a taxi, got in, and gave the driver the name of our hotel. We drove in silence all the way, not sulking, nor in anger. Obviously, that was the way it was going to be with the geishas. Later, I found out that Marlon had been correct about geisha behavior in every detail but one. As I suppose everyone has learned by this time, real geishas—and these were real—don't screw your ears off. They just talk.

I was already planning the rest of the evening in my head. When Marlon left me to keep his nine-o'clock appointment, I intended to go to the Ginza, find myself a bogus geisha, and feed—not on apples, tea, and cookies, but on slices of raw tuna marinated in soy sauce and horseradish, drink double shots of fine Japanese whiskey, and, after that, take my almond-eyed darling to bed, and get my ears screwed off.

CHAPTER FOURTEEN

AFTER A WEEK in Tokyo
we left for location in Kyoto, the Jewel of Japan. We stayed
at the Miyako Hotel, which was situated atop a hill. From our
windows, we had a panoramic view of that lovely city of
temples. Marlon chose to live in a suite furnished in the traditional Japanese style. I was never comfortable squatting on a
pillow on the floor, eating at a low table. My legs cramped and
my back ached for want of support, so I chose to live in a
Western-style suite.

At first I thought it was my imagination, but in fact everything—chairs, beds, tables, whatever—were scaled down in
order to accommodate smaller people. When I looked in the

bathroom mirror, I had to bend a little to see the top of my head. I stooped more than usual when I was washing my hands in the water basin, and I squatted lower than I was accustomed to when I sat on the toilet seat.

The first few days of shooting on location passed uneventfully, and Marlon soon grew bored. From the start, he believed that *Sayonara* was a wide-screen Technicolor travelogue, pumped up with an improbable love story.

One day we were walking toward the set, dragging our heels and not talking, when Marlon turned to me suddenly and said, out of his churning thoughts, "I will not say, 'Look at the carp!' Nor will I say, 'Look at the bridge!' Or 'Look at that cock!'"

"Look at *what* cock," I said. "Whose cock?"

"Josh has found a white cock with a tail twenty feet long. For some reason, the Japanese breed these long-tailed cocks. Anyway, he wants a shot of the cock, and he wants me to say, 'Look at that cock!' so he'll have a reason to cut to it. He's seen a bridge he'd like to photograph, too, so he wants me to say, 'Look at that bridge!' For God's sake, Freddie, what are we filming? A travelogue or a motion picture? And what am I? An actor, or a guide for tourists? As far as I'm concerned, Logan can take the cock and shove it. Twenty-foot tail and all."

"Well, why don't you suggest some script changes and give those shitty lines to another actor? To Red Buttons, maybe. Or James Garner. They want to pad their parts, and they'll love you for the extra lines."

Marlon laughed his head off. It was a good example, he told me, of my fine Italian hand, sticking in the shiv.

"What do you think of Logan as a director?" he asked when he had stopped laughing.

Director Joshua Logan, Marlon, and producer William Goetz on the Sayonara *set.* (WARNER BROS. PICTURES INC.)

"I think it's too early to tell," I said. "He may be a crafts-man—maybe, I don't know. But an artist? I don't think so."

"I'm going to test him in this next shot," Marlon said.

The scene was with Red Buttons and several Japanese children. It was the exterior of a house on the canal, the home of Buttons and his Oriental wife. On the way to visit him, Marlon stops to comb his hair, indulges in some horseplay with the kids, then he is met by Red. After an exchange of greetings, they go indoors and the scene ends. Without projecting any emotion at all, Marlon made "faces" (expressions inappropriate to the text), and to his surprise Logan thought he was "just marvelous" and ordered the take printed. After that, Marlon didn't trust his director's opinion, and he himself selected the take he thought was best to print.

By this time, diarrhea, the usual travelers' complaint, was running rampant in the company. Marlon is a born traveler and is apparently immune to radical changes in diet and drinking water that give nearly everybody else trouble from time to time. But this time he claimed to have the trots so that he could take a day off and relieve the tedium of work.

We worked lackadaisically through an afternoon on the script of *Vermilion*, sipping sweetened tea and gossiping. In the evening, about seven-thirty, the phone rang and Marlon answered. The desk clerk informed him that Mr. Truman Capote was on his way up to see him. Marlon hung up and said, "Shit! I forgot all about the interview with Capote. He's traveling here with Cecil Beaton, and I promised him he could see me."

"I'd like to meet him," I said. "I hear he's quite a character."

"Okay, but split soon after. Let's scatter a lot of pages around the pad. Make it look as though we were in the middle of some heavy work and pretend we have to get back to working on the script later tonight. After you leave, call me every hour or so, then I'll have an excuse to cut the interview short if I want to."

Quickly we placed stacked pages of script on the table, on the sleeping mat, on the floor, all over the place. Here and there we scattered writing pads and pencils, placed a tape recorder in full view, and rolled a discarded page of text onto the carriage of an empty typewriter. All in all, the setting gave the impression of a couple of screenwriters who had been holed up for weeks to meet an important deadline.

There was a knock, and the maid opened the door. Capote stood there, posed on the threshold, framed in the doorway. He made a very pretty picture. He was dressed in harmonic tawny tones: desert shoes, corduroy trousers of light brown, and a tan cardigan sweater of thick wool. He moved into the room with that odd, graceful gait of his, cradling a bottle of vodka in the crook of his arm. I had heard that Capote was small, but I was surprised to see how really small he was. He was slim and trim as a boy, and his feet and hands were as tiny as a child's. Although he was thirty years old or more, he had the frank gaze and smooth features of a twelve-year-old innocent. I had never heard him speak, and the high-pitched nasality of his voice softly slurring the words gave me the feeling that an amateur ventriloquist was speaking through this smaller-than-life-size but perfectly proportioned doll.

Neither I nor anyone else, however, would dare to laugh or smile in ridicule of his figure or speech. It was too well known that behind those baby-blue eyes there was a quick intelligence that could cripple you with the spoken word, or murder you with the written one.

Capote lifted the bottle of vodka nestled in his arm and with great care placed it in the center of the low table. Marlon asked the maid to bring a bucket of ice cubes. I was introduced, and then we all had some small talk about the Japanese cuisine, the anachronistic ceremonies of the culture, and its exquisite customs.

Abruptly, out of nowhere, Capote began to relate a strange and fascinating story. He and Leonard Bernstein loved to gossip about their friends, he said, and one day, while they were alone together in the conductor's apartment, they had themselves a hell of a time cutting up mutual acquaintances. Bernstein had hidden a microphone somewhere in the room, and not knowing everything he said was going on the tape, Capote spoke freely about the faults and vices of everyone in their crowd. If he slowed down a little, Bernstein prodded him to reveal the more intimate details of current scandals involving their friends. Happily, Capote obliged him.

Not long after, Capote attended a party in Bernstein's house. Everyone in their set was present, including nearly all the people he had been talking about so freely that day alone with Lennie. Although the party was obviously a huge success without any adornment, Bernstein was going around telling everybody that he was going to give them a surprise later on, a rare treat, something they would never forget.

At the height of the party, Bernstein called for attention and announced he was ready to present his surprise. The crowd settled down in quiet anticipation. A tape recorder was produced, and the host pressed the playback button himself. The suddenly hushed room was filled with Capote's distinctive voice, repeating everything he had confided to Bernstein that day. Worse, the tape had been edited so that only his side of the dialogue was heard.

"Why, it was a monologue in maliciousness," Capote recalled.

The guests were stunned to hear themselves so attacked by

[182]

one they had considered an old friend, and at first they directed their shock and anger toward Capote as the tape ground on. But then they turned away from him, when the shock wore off, and concentrated on Bernstein. In various ways, they told him it was a bad joke, if it was meant to be one, and he was the only one who was laughing. The trick had backfired.

That was the end of the story. I wondered why Capote had told it. What was the point? Was he trying to tell Marlon something? I looked at my friend, trying to read him, and saw him shake his head with sympathy for Capote at being made the butt of a cruel put-on.

I felt a little stupid. I didn't know how to react, or what to say, or what kind of face to make. But the story, and Capote's arriving with the vodka, made me suspicious. I had a strong foreboding that Capote, after he had gained Marlon's confidence, would chop him up into small pieces, then go around telling people that mayhem was the writer's art.

It was eight o'clock when I left them. As Marlon and I had agreed, I split as soon as it was convenient. At loose ends, I called Miiko Taka, *Sayonara*'s leading lady, and we went to a discotheque on Kyoto's main drag to listen to American jazz and have a drink or two. Miiko was an attractive Nisei who spoke Japanese fluently and graciously acted as my interpreter and guide.

At the appointed time, an hour later, I called Marlon and was a little alarmed to find him already as high as the proverbial kite. He spoke rapidly, sixteen to the dozen, rattling along with all his defenses down. He rarely drank, and sometimes, after only a drink or two, his natural distrust of strangers would evaporate and he would be sentimental, maudlin, and ready to unfold the story of his life, freely trotting out all the

Miiko Taka and Marlon as they appear in Sayonara.
(WARNER BROS. PICTURES INC.)

skeletons in his closet. Occasionally, I had even seen him high
when he hadn't even taken a drink. Good conversation was
enough to release the adrenalin, intoxicate him, and loosen his
tongue. And anyone who had ever heard Capote in action knew
that he was a fascinating conversationalist.

[184]

"Have you been drinking?" I asked Marlon.

"What? No, of course not. What makes you ask that?" He sounded indignant.

"You sound a little high, so I figured you had some of that vodka Capote brought."

"I had a couple of nips, that's all."

"Be cool, man," I said. "Don't say anything you might regret later."

"Truman's already gotten his interview. We're just chatting now, *entre nous*. Which means, just between us, off the record, not for publication, you ignorant wop."

That piece of information made me all the more suspicious.

"Sometimes 'off the record' means the actual interview has only just begun," I said. "So cool it, man. Why chance it?"

"Call me in an hour," he said impatiently and hung up.

An hour passed and I called again. He sounded even higher than before, babbling like a swift-flowing stream, and there was nothing I could do to dam it up.

"Miiko has an early call for tomorrow," I said, "and I'm taking her home. If you want me, I'll be in my room."

"Right," Marlon said and clicked off, obviously anxious to resume his conversation.

I went back to the hotel with Miiko, we said good night, and I went to my room, got into bed, and fell asleep.

About two-thirty in the morning, the telephone woke me up again. It was Marlon, still flying high and wanting company. I told him I was too wiped out for company, or work, or anything else, so we decided to call it a night. It wasn't the end of the story, though. That would come later.

Meanwhile, the filming of *Sayonara* went on. Marlon was portraying a character named Major Gruver, and the part had originally been written "straight," without dialect. It was Marlon's idea, however, to play the major with a Southern accent. He once told me that using an accent puts into play particular muscles of the face, which in turn affect the expressions and features of the actor, helping him to project the character he is depicting with greater force. I could understand that all right, but I advised him that superimposing an accent on a character that was conceived and written "straight" presented certain problems. Some of the dialogue would have to be changed and many of the lines would have to be cut out entirely.

"Like what, for instance?" Marlon said.

"Well, in that scene with Jim Garner, when you explain that you never wanted to be a military officer, that you really wanted to be an actor, but your father, who is a four-star general, and his father a general before him, put the pressure on you and threatened to disown you if you persisted in pursuing your theatrical career—"

"Get to the point," Marlon interrupted. "Don't be such a windbag."

"You say that you got the acting bug at West Point while you were playing in a student production of a play written by Molnar." I paused for his reaction.

Marlon looked at me, perplexed. "Well, go on."

"Don't you get it?"

"Frankly, no."

"Molnar was a Hungarian playwright who wrote witty, sophisticated dialogue."

"So?"

"So acting with a Southern accent in a Molnar play, especially in that salt-pork-and-black-eyed-peas accent you're using, is as silly as playing Shakespeare with a stutter. No wonder your four-star general father threatened to disown you. If he saw you in that Molnar play, he must have thought he'd spawned some kind of new, unique nut. . . . Say, some-

[186]

James Garner, Miiko Taka, and the author.

thing just occurred to me. You've never heard of Molnar, have you?"

"Well, he was never very big in Nebraska."

"Holy shit! And I believed that you could never, *would* never say a line unless you knew exactly, precisely what it meant. Boy, was I wrong!"

"I suppose all this horseshit is leading up to something. What is it? And please be brief."

"Let's change the lines. Say you wanted to be a painter instead of an Air Force pilot. Or you wanted to be an author. A lot of well-known authors come from the South."

"No, let's keep the lines in, intact. I like the idea that he wanted to leave West Point to become an actor. I can relate to that."

"All right. But then change the name of the playwright. Instead of Molnar, say Eugene O'Neill, or Lillian Hellman. Then the Southern accent might be plausible."

"But I *like* the implausibility of it. Maybe you're not entirely wrong, though. I'll add a line or two for insurance."

"Add what line or two?"

"I don't know yet. I'll think of something during the scene. Now, no more. Let's talk about something else."

What Marlon usually wanted to talk about was girls, and on the set of *Sayonara*, not to mention off the set, there was plenty to talk about. I think we must have fucked almost every Japanese girl involved with the picture. One was unusually tall for a Japanese, a luscious girl with big tits. She looked twenty-two, but she was really only seventeen. I saw her casting flirtatious eyes at me one day on the set, and by that night we were in bed. When she first kissed me, she demonstrated a talent I didn't know she had. Her deep kiss was so deep, so absorbing, so like a vacuum cleaner, that she nearly drew my tongue out by the roots. If I had been a masochist, I could have appreciated it a lot more because it hurt like hell.

I told Marlon about the girl (not about the kiss) and he said, "Give me a taste of that."

"Okay," I said. I thought I'd let him find out the rest for himself.

"How did you make out?" I asked him next morning. Marlon just glared at me. His mouth was bitten and his tongue swollen so badly that he could scarcely work that day. He mumbled his way through the lines, and it was pretty much a total loss.

In subsequent dates, I would have said ordinarily that he was taking revenge except that it was the way he always behaved with my girls. In this case, everything was complicated by the different standards of Japanese women.

I had taken an actress in the cast back to her room in our hotel one night when we encountered Marlon in the hall while we were on the way to her room. She invited him in for a friendly nightcap, and we sat around talking and drinking for a little while. Then Marlon got up, stretched, and began to take off his clothes.

"Well, good night, Freddie," he said.

I was furious. "What do you mean, good night?" I said. "I was here first."

"But I'm here now," he said. "Good night, Freddie."

He went right on undressing and calmly insisted that he was going to stay there for the night. My little friend was terribly embarrassed, and rather than make a scene about it, I left. Marlon took her out several times after that for dinner, and if it was any consolation, she sneaked out after every date with him and came to me.

Fairly early in the picture I began to see girls always standing around the set, primping and smiling and talking to the crew.

"Who are these girls?" I asked Logan curiously.

"I understand they go around with the soundmen," he said. "Their girls, I suppose."

I couldn't believe that and went over to a pair of the best-looking ones and began making a pitch to them, while they smiled and giggled, in the Japanese way. One soundman came over to me and said genially, "Sorry, but we're taking these two out to dinner tonight. I understand, though, that they've got a very nice friend. Maybe we could all go out together tomorrow night." I agreed and the arrangements were made.

The friend turned out to be the loveliest girl I had met in

Japan, an exquisite thing named Masako. The six of us went to dinner and had a fine time. I was enchanted with Masako, and I could see she felt the same way. Halfway through dinner, the girls started whispering to each other and soon they were collapsing in fits of giggling. They asked to be excused and rushed to the ladies' room, still convulsed.

"What's the matter with *them*," I whispered to Masako when they returned.

"Oh, they think it is very funny," she said. "Very funny. They all got their periods at the same time today."

I don't know how funny my friends thought it was, but I didn't care. Masako and I had really hit it off, and we began to go steady, as the saying once went.

Inevitably, and as always, Marlon discovered Masako too, and I heard his familiar line, "How about giving me a taste of that?"

This time I *did* care, but I tried not to make an issue of it. "I don't know," I said. "I think she's in love with me. You know how these Japanese girls are. They stay with one man. And they don't give a damn about movie stars."

It was as though I hadn't said anything. "Why don't you ask her for dinner in my suite, the three of us, then you excuse yourself when you have the opportunity and go back to your room?"

I hated to do that to Masako, and to myself, but there didn't seem to be anything to do except agree.

We had dinner with Marlon in his suite, as planned. Masako seemed surprised there were only three of us; obviously, she had expected a foursome. She might have thought it a little strange, too, that Marlon appeared in a Japanese bathrobe, as though he were measuring the shortest distance to bed.

After a splendid dinner and a good deal of sake, I could

feel myself getting stoned, and that seemed a good enough excuse (I hardly needed any more) to excuse myself, stagger back to my room, and fall on the bed, where I promptly fell asleep.

Masako had a key to my room, because she sometimes stayed with me, and about two hours later she shook me awake. She was in tears.

"Marlon told me you had this all planned and you wanted me to stay with him. Is it true?"

I felt miserable, but I had to admit it was. I couldn't explain it to myself, much less to her.

For the next few days Masako appeared infrequently. She looked sad and ashamed. Then she disappeared for a while. I think both Marlon and I realized then what a gem she was, and we missed her. A few days later, she was back on the set.

"What are you doing?" I asked her.

"I got a job working in your picture," she said calmly.

"Will you come out with me tonight?"

"I'm sorry, I can't. I'm going with one of the camera operators. He's that one, right over there."

I looked where she was pointing and couldn't believe it. He was at least fifty and didn't look like much of a swinger.

"Oh, come on, Masako," I said. "Go out with me tonight."

"No, we are all through," she said firmly.

"Well, best of luck, then," I said.

Later that night, while I was going to my room, I encountered her running down the corridor, in tears again.

"What's the matter, Masako?" I said, catching her and holding her.

"It's Marlon," she sobbed. "He got me into his room on some excuse I believed, and then he tried to get me into bed. I had to fight him off."

"I don't think he'll try that anymore," I tried to reassure

*The author's wedding, showing the author and his bride Marcia,
her parents, the minister, Anna Kashfi, and Marlon
clowning with a camera.*

her, without much conviction. She calmed down a little, and we said good night.

"What's the matter with you?" I said to Marlon next day. "Why did you do that to Masako? She's a nice girl. She just wants a guy she can be true to, and obviously you and I aren't it. She's no tramp, man."

He just looked sad, didn't try to explain (there wasn't anything to explain, really), and I think he felt ashamed because he saw to it that Masako got a bit part in the picture, for more money. From that time until the end of the filming, he treated her like a lady.

After several months of shooting, the Japanese exteriors were in the can, and the company prepared to return to Hollywood to film the interiors. Everyone was sorry to leave Japan. The Japanese are really an emotional people, and when they like you, they fall in love with you—as I had seen with Masako. There was much shedding of tears when we left, and as corny as it may sound, a lot of *"sayonaras."*

After Japan, Hollywood seemed very strange, but Marcia was waiting eagerly for me, as Anna was for Marlon. While we had been away, the two girls had come to be intimate friends, as we had expected.

"I'm going to marry Marcia," I told Marlon.

"Do you know what you're doing?" he said, looking very serious.

"Yes. And I want you to be best man. Marcia wants Anna to be maid of honor." It was agreed.

The ceremony was to take place at the home of Marcia's parents in Hollywood. You would have thought it was Marlon's wedding. Because he doesn't like pictures, he insisted that there be no photographers if he was going to be best man.

"But Marcia wants pictures of the whole thing," I protested.

"I'll take the pictures," Marlon promised.

"You don't mind if the preacher is there, do you?" I asked sarcastically.

He ignored it. "Don't worry," he said, "I'll take the pictures."

In the end, there was one other photographer. Marcia's old-maid aunt appeared, carrying an early Kodak. As it happened, the aunt was a lush, but she lurched around merrily, taking pictures. Marlon was taking pictures too, as he had promised, and I took a few with his camera. The old aunt got more than anybody, though. She shot Marlon taking pictures, took every group in sight, then Brando and Anna, then more groups.

Fortunately for everybody, she was very busy, because when I asked Marlon later how the wedding pictures came out, he said blandly, "I had an accident with them, Freddie. They were all exposed. I must have done it when I was taking the rolls out of the camera."

I should have known. But the maiden aunt had a lot of them, and although some were as out of focus as she had been, we did have a fairly good picture record of the wedding.

It was quite a contrast when Marlon and Anna got married, not long after. It was quick and secret and without any publicity until it was over. For one thing, Anna was pregnant. She had told Marcia, "If you ever want to get pregnant, it's easy. I studied the cycle, and look what happened to me."

I did what I could to prevent the marriage, which was exactly nothing as far as effectiveness was concerned. When Marlon told me he had made up his mind, I said, "You shouldn't marry her. That's my feeling."

"But you told me she was the best one I'd ever had. Remember?"

"I remember, but I've changed my mind. I don't think you should."

I put up an argument about it, and I think Marlon had just about decided he wasn't going to do it when she told him she was pregnant and wanted to have the baby. That was the only way to get Marlon down the aisle, as Movita later discovered.

CHAPTER FIFTEEN

SAYONARA was nearing completion in Hollywood when Josh Logan approached Marlon on the set one day, his generous girth shaking with agitation.

"Marlon, you remember that interview in Japan with Capote? Well, I've just read the galleys. Everything—everything—that was said between you two will be published in *The New Yorker*."

Remembering what he had said to Capote about Logan's ability as a director, Marlon went pale under his makeup. Naturally, Logan was hurt when he read what had been said about him. He didn't want the world to know that Marlon, whom he had declared freely was America's finest actor, held him in such low esteem as a director.

As for Marlon, he was shaken by Capote's betrayal. He went directly to his dressing room when Logan told him the news and wrote a letter to Capote, pleading with him to delete the unkind things he had said about his colleagues, his family, and his friends. Capote could say anything he wanted to about him, he said, but he begged that the others would be left out of it. He also reminded Capote about his promise that certain parts of their talk would be off the record and not to be published.

The letter was a waste of time. Capote never bothered to answer it.

Years later, in an interview with a reporter for the magazine section of the *Los Angeles Times*, he was quoted as saying: "I realized that the most banal thing in journalism would be an interview with a film star, so I put a number of names in a hat and pulled out, God knows why, Marlon Brando. . . . So I went to Japan (where Marlon was making *Sayonara*) and spent the prescribed time—one evening—and then spent a year on the piece because it had to be perfection, because my part was to take this banal thing and turn it into *a work of art*. Lots of people can't understand why I wrote it. He sent me the *long*est, most con*fused* letter. . . ."

The piece was called, "The Duke in His Domain," and it was published in *The New Yorker*. It was a work of art, all right. It was also a masterpiece of maliciousness, condescension, and simple deceit.

When the shooting on *Sayonara* was completed at last, and the scenes were assembled, Marlon and I attended a private screening of the rough cut at Warners studios. Everyone who had been concerned with the production was there: Bill Goetz,

Sam Gilman, the Brandos, along with the unseen Fiores
off for a weekend of fun in San Francisco. (The photos
were taken by the author's wife.)

Logan, film editors, publicity men, front-office bigwigs, and so on.

As the picture began to unfold, everyone seemed enraptured by it before it was a third through. Marlon's Southern accent was precisely on target, and it had the ring of authenticity. The picture had the look of a box-office blockbuster, and the money men were ecstatic. It appeared certain to bring in millions upon millions in profit. Who cared that it was banal beyond belief? Or that the hopped-up color photography was unbearably Christmasy? Or that lovely Japan was made to look like a country designed by Disney?

Then the scene I had been waiting for came on the screen. In his thick accent, Marlon was confessing to James Garner that he wanted to quit West Point to become an actor, but his four-star-general father forced him to remain in the army. Marlon's dialogue, and the lines he had told me he was going to add, went something like this: "Ah got the actin' bug at Wes' Poin' w'ile playin' a paht inna play by Molnar." On screen, Marlon paused and gazed at the ground in thought. Then he looked up at Garner again and went on: "You've nevah heard Molnar played with a Southern accent, have ya? Well, ah'll tell ya, it wuz somethin' to behold."

To my surprise, there wasn't a single laugh from the audience. They simply waited for his next line. Marlon and I looked at each other and broke up. Several people in the audience turned around with stern, shushing looks, but when they saw who was laughing, the admonishing glares turned to benevolent smiles. No doubt they thought Marlon and I were sharing some harmless, private joke, because they could never have believed that even the impish Brando would laugh at his own movie.

So everyone was happy and *Sayonara* was released for the Christmas season in 1957. It got split reviews from the critics, understandably, but the first impression of the screening was confirmed by the exhibitors. It was going to be a box-office smash.

I was shaving one morning when Marlon came into my apartment and stormed into the bathroom, ready to bite my head off.

"What's the matter?" I said, a little alarmed.

He slammed a copy of *The New Yorker* on my side table, stabbed at it with his index finger and said, "Page eighty-four. Read it!"

I wiped the soap off my face, picked up the magazine, turned to page eighty-four, and saw a review of *Sayonara* by John McCarten, titled "Variation on the Puccini Caper." I began to read: "Among the innumerable credits that spin past your eyes before the film *Sayonara* settles down to describing the hazardous course of love between U. S. military personnel and indigenous beauties in Japan is one containing the information that Marlon Brando, the star of the proceedings, was coached in dialogue by Carlo Fiori [sic]. As you will discover if you see *Sayonara*—and I hope you do—Mr. Fiori ranks right up there with Professor Higgins in the art of imposing speech patterns upon a susceptible subject. Instead of mumbling along in his customary Middle Western style, Mr. Brando, under the guidance of Mr. Fiori, mumbles along with a corn-pone-and-chitlin accent that seems absolutely legitimate, even to the generic drawback of occasionally—particularly when he is cracking jokes—making him sound like the end man in a minstrel show. . . ."

I was a little annoyed to see my name misspelled (it had also been misspelled in the screen credits), but I was no longer annoyed about that, and I laughed.

"Is he a friend of yours?" Marlon demanded.

"If he were a friend, I'd drop him for misspelling my name."

"I asked you—is he a friend of yours?"

"And I just told you, no, I never met the man."

"Then why did he give you the credit for my Southern accent?"

"It was his way of spoofing the movie, and the tone of his review was absolutely perfect, I thought. You've got to admit that's one crazy screen credit—Carlo Fiore, dialogue coach to Mr. Marlon Brando. Anyway, you knew *Sayonara* was a soap opera all the time. You can't expect an intelligent critic to treat it seriously. Or do you?"

Marlon realized that his suspicions, whatever they might have been, were unfounded. He didn't know what to say.

"I'll write to McCarten," I said, "and tell him that I had nothing to do with your using a Southern accent. I'll say that in fact I was against your using an accent from the beginning."

"No, no. Don't trouble yourself about it. Just forget it."

"No trouble," I said. "I'll just drop him a note."

"I said *no*," Marlon shouted. "That's one of your faults. You always blow things out of proportion."

With *Sayonara* out of the way, we went back to working on the first draft of *Burst of Vermilion*. When we got it together, it was 240 pages of rambling and sometimes almost incoherent dialogue. I wanted to tighten it up a little before we submitted it to Paramount.

"No, I'll submit it as it is," Marlon said.

"But it's way, way too long. There are big holes in it, barren stretches leading nowhere. Let's take a week or two and edit and polish it. As it is, they'll nay-say us, sure as shootin'," I said, Western style.

"Listen, man," Marlon said, "nobody's going to vote it

down, 'cause I got the vote that *counts.* Just you watch. They'll like it."

So the script was given to Paramount as it stood, and I spent a restless week nervously chewing up the rug, waiting for a response. Marlon brought the bad news. He came over to my place and sat on the sofa, looking glum.

"Thumbs down, huh?" I said.

"It was no, no, no, right down the line."

"I told you we should have polished it, tightened it, or something."

Suddenly Marlon dropped down on the floor and rolled with laughter. "I read the script again. As though I was reading it for the first time—through their eyes. Wow! Was it lousy!"

"What are you going to do now?"

He stood up, composed himself, and shrugged. "Keep searching for a script, I guess."

"Have you got any idea what you want?"

"Yeah, kinda. Something like *The Count of Monte Cristo* on a horse."

Nevertheless, we were getting nowhere fast trying to develop a script for the Western, and Marlon thought it would be a good time to pay off the remainder of his debt to Zanuck. He had agreed to star in *The Young Lions,* and after that he would be free to give his full attention to his own projects.

As for me, I was finding more and more work as an actor during Marlon's long layoffs, going from "extra" work to bit parts, then to featured roles and second leads. It was gratifying to know I could earn at least a decent living as an actor in television and movies. But acting bored me. The scripts I was given to read were so atrocious I found it almost impossible to memorize my lines. I had no ambition, no drive, no real desire to be famous or rich. I was adrift and didn't care that I was adrift.

Marlon scolded me. "Goddammit, Freddie, you're like a dog tugging at the leash. When I want you for work, I've always got to tow you in."

"I know, I know," I said. "But instead of bugging me about it, tell me what I can do."

"See a psychiatrist."

"Oh, shit! Here we go again. I'm not ready for psychiatry yet."

"Of course you are. You're on a sinking ship and you'd better take the plunge or drown. Don't you know that lack of energy and ambition are only the symptoms of a deep emotional problem? A good psychiatrist can help you."

"Has psychiatry helped you?"

"Of course it has. Why do you think I continue in analysis? Without it I'd have gone off my rocker. The guys in white jackets would have put me away a long time ago."

"Okay," I said. "I'll give it a try, I promise. I'll give it a real, serious try. But without my insanity, I'll have no excuse for my failure. I'll have to face the fact that I have a spectacular lack of talent, and I'll want to cut my throat. And it'll be your fault."

Marlon gave me a small, twisted smile, the kind he always gave when he was slightly embarrassed. "You can begin in analysis when you get back from Europe," he said.

"Europe?"

"Yeah. I want you to come with me as dialogue coach in *The Young Lions*. I'm changing the Nazi heel into a kind of tragic hero. I'm gonna do a complete about-face in the interpretation of the character, and it'll be a lot of work. I'll need some help."

[203]

When I thought about that conversation later, I realized that psychiatry had done at least one thing for Marlon. He could come out of the somewhat unreal world he lived in and deal with the real one when he had to. When we were finishing the final shots for *Sayonara*, Marlon had gone up to the roof of the studio one hot day during the lunch hour to take a sunbath. The sun was really pouring down, and seeing two faucets sticking out of the roof, Marlon turned one on to wet himself with the water and cool off.

Within a few minutes, the studio was surrounded by firetrucks. Marlon turned the water off and went down to find out what the excitement was about.

The fire captain, a very tough Irishman, was angry and asking questions of everybody. "Who's been up on the roof?" he wanted to know. Brando identified himself and admitted that he had been there.

The captain strode over to him belligerently. He looked like a man who wasn't impressed by movie stars; maybe he'd heard of Marlon's Hollywood reputation as a smart ass, which he was trying to live down.

"Did you turn a faucet up there?"

"Sure," Marlon said. "I wanted to cool myself off."

"Well, you turned on a fire alarm when you did that, and while we were on the way here, we had an accident and one of my men got hurt."

Marlon looked him right in the eye. "I'm sorry about that," he said, "but how was I to know it was a fire alarm?"

"There's a sign there," the captain snapped. "Can't you guys read?"

Marlon kept his temper. "There isn't any sign up there," he said. "You can go and see for yourself."

We all trooped up to the roof. Sure enough, there wasn't any sign, anywhere, and it was the captain's turn to be embarrassed. There had been too many witnesses, however. George Glass, the studio's public-relations man, hurried to the nearest telephone and called a friend on one of the newspapers. "Do me a favor and kill that story," I could hear him saying. And in fact, it never appeared. I heard that the studio had put all its powerful influence behind the suppression.

Still, I thought, if he's so smart, why can't he see what he's getting into with Anna? They weren't married yet, but I was getting occasional glimpses of future trouble. I had gone to the movies one night with them (I don't remember why Marcia wasn't there), and another couple had come along, an MCA executive and his wife, a very old friend who had been like an affectionate aunt to Marlon. She was an attractive woman, and Marlon was obviously fond of her. I could see Anna watching them, and the murderous jealousy that always seemed to be just below the surface of her lovely face was in her eyes. I thought, She's beginning to crack a little.

Marlon had to get away from her, from time to time, so that he could breathe a little and pursue his usual interests, which meant balling chicks who had caught his fancy. He asked me to go with him to New York one day on the pretext of business; we would be staying at the Plaza, as usual, he said. I knew why he wanted to go. His current interest was France Nuyen, the Eurasian actress, who at the moment happened to be in New York, playing in the stage version of *The World of Suzie Wong*.

They had had an affair that lasted nearly a year before it broke up. But Marlon couldn't let her go. He heard she was engaged to a psychiatrist and immediately called her up for a date. She agreed, and Marlon hung up the phone, delighted.

"Why don't you leave her alone and stop meddling with her life?" I said to him as we were on our way to New York.

"I guess it's my vanity," he answered honestly. "I still

France Nuyen on a date with Marlon. (WIDE WORLD PHOTOS)

want to believe I'm top man. And then there's the other thing."

"What other thing?"

"With women, I've got a long bamboo pole with a leather loop on the end of it. I slip the loop around their necks so that they can't get away or come too close. Like catching snakes."

I couldn't blame him for looping France. She was of mixed Chinese and French parentage, a lovely dark girl with a beautiful ass—the Brando prerequisite. He is a legs-and-ass man. As every feminist who has read this far must understand by now, if she hasn't chewed up the book in sheer rage, Marlon is also the ultimate Male Chauvinist Pig.

In New York, he wouldn't let me out of his sight except when France was free and he could see her. She sat at his feet, looking up at him adoringly, in the female Asian manner. But as Caucasian men have often discovered, underneath the Oriental sweetness she was as tough as nails, a determined, opinionated woman who had a weakness for Marlon. While she was having it, I was free to go down to the Village and elsewhere around New York, looking up old acquaintances and seeing my jazz musician friends. During France's performances, Marlon and I would sit in the Plaza, working in a desultory way on a new script for *Vermilion*, but we made little progress. Our minds were elsewhere.

Back in Hollywood, it was nearly time to go to Europe for *The Young Lions.*

"I'm going to take Marcia with me," I said to Marlon.

"No, no, you can't do that," he said. "It's going to be all work. No wives."

"She'll be terribly disappointed."

"I can't help it. That's the way it's going to be."

I told Marcia the bad news, and we had a violent quarrel.

"Tell him you won't go unless I come," she insisted.

"I can't do that," I said.

"If you go without me," Marcia said, "I'm going to leave you and go back to New York."

She did, too, but she came back again, and our marriage lasted about two years, before she left me for good this time and got a job in Los Angeles in the fashion business, which she knew so well. Tragically, she was killed in an automobile crash as she was driving to Palm Springs. Marlon came to the funeral and could hardly have been sweeter to me. He saw to it that I wasn't alone when, for the first time, I desperately needed someone near me.

When we parted that first time, over Marlon's refusal to let her go to Europe, I felt badly enough, but I will have to admit I was excited about the trip. It was spring when we went to France to begin shooting, and spring in Paris was exactly as advertised.

Before shooting began, we had a few days to enjoy Paris. Marlon and I went to dinner with Dean Martin and Montgomery Clift. Since I had kicked drugs, I was drinking heavily—not to get drunk but to tranquilize myself. To me, alcohol was a pain-relieving, soothing medication. The amount of whiskey I could put away without getting drunk never failed to amaze Marlon, and he goaded me and Clift, who was something of a heavy drinker himself, into a drinking bout.

Dean Martin would have none of it. Dino has the reputation of being a heavy drinker, but he hardly drinks at all. It's a running gag, like Jack Benny's stinginess. Dino is satisfied with nursing and fondling a single Cinzano all night. One of his old cronies—I think it was Phil Harris—has said, "Dean Martin a drinker? Why, I *spill* more than he *drinks*."

I lost the drinking bout to Clift. The last thing I remembered next day was Dino hailing a cab, Marlon and Clift supporting me to the taxi, and my falling to my knees and passing out while I was crawling in. About four hours later, I came to

Montgomery Clift, Marlon, and Dean Martin on the
set of The Young Lions.

in my hotel room, vaguely aware of Marlon nursing me with
ice packs, full of apologies and trying to placate me with
sweet talk.

"You and your childish games," I said. "Those crazy fucking contests you keep goading me into will do me in some day."

In the cocktail lounge of the Hotel Prince de Galles, that
first week, Marlon had a booming quarrel with Liliane
Montevecchi, his leading lady in *The Young Lions*. Liliane was
a beautiful, passionate, hot-tempered young lady. To empha-
size a point in her argument, she slammed her hand down on
the table and accidentally knocked a boiling hot pot of tea
onto Marlon's lap. He leaped up screaming, and while he was
still in the air, it seemed, he pulled down his pants, which
were soaked with the tea that had scalded his crotch, and ran
bare-ass out of the lounge. The fashionable clientele observed

his exit as nothing more than another Brando eccentricity and scarcely moved a muscle. Shrugging their shoulders eloquently, they went back to their own conversations.

Soon after, I went to Marlon's room in the Hotel Raphael and found him lying nude, spread-eagled on the bed, while a doctor smeared a sulphur-yellow salve on his blistered cock and balls. I had never seen him look so woebegone in my life, ever.

"This would have to happen *now*," he lamented, in a sad, rasping voice. "Right smack in the middle of Paris, it's spring, and here I am with my prick in a sling."

Next day Marlon appeared on the set ready to go to work, resplendent in his Nazi uniform and with his genitals wrapped in surgical gauze. It was a sorry sight to see him shuffling along to hit his marks before the camera, his legs apart, walking as though he were wearing snow shoes.

It was long enough after the war, but when the French found out that the Nazi in *The Young Lions* had been transformed into a tragic hero, they gave the company a bad time.

While we were filming inside an actual concentration camp in Alsace-Lorraine, the French crew struck because the American crew worked naked to the waist, smoked, and played little jokes to break the tedium of the labor. The French were indignant at the Americans' behavior, saying that they weren't displaying the proper respect for the victims who had suffered and died there. So that work could be resumed, the American crew put out their cigarettes and wore shirts over their sweat-drenched torsos. I admired their patience. I was sure that if the circumstances had been more convenient they wouldn't have let pass some of the remarks the French were passing about them.

Things were tense for a while, but I saw only one serious altercation. During a lunch break, a member of our crew complained to the French caterer that he had ordered the beef and was brought chicken instead, whereupon the caterer discharged a barrage of insults in French. The American was a quiet, mild man, but his temper had been held in check too long. Red with rage and without rising from his chair, he hit the rude waiter with a terrific left hook to the groin. The waiter cupped his balls in his hand and ran doubled up to the kitchen. From that moment, the manners of the French caterers improved noticeably.

The work went much better than the catering. Marlon is the darling of all the film editors and cutters who work on his movies. The scenes of a motion picture are not filmed sequentially but are shot in widely separated segments which are later assembled to make a whole. Sometimes a key scene that occurs in the middle of the scenario is filmed on the first day of shooting, and in order to give that scene its proper value, an actor, in his mind's eye, must see the performance in its entirety, from beginning to end, so that the scene will fit neatly into place, like the pieces of a jigsaw puzzle. An actor must have this sense of proportion—the capacity to view things in their true relations, or relative importance—or give up acting entirely.

Of course, it is true that a good director might lend this ability to an imperfect actor, to extract a decent performance from him, but in the long run, for a career of any length, an actor must stand alone. Marlon possesses this sense of perspective to a spectacular degree, and when the film editors splice his scrambled scenes and join them in sequence, they fit together with the exactness of a precision machine.

For example, the first scene photographed in *The Young Lions* was located in a small town in France that was being besieged by the advancing Germans. Marlon, as a young officer, was in command of a company entrenched in a ditch, and

Director Edward Dmytryk, Marlon, and technicians
Joe McDonald and Ben Chapman.

he gave the order to fire upon the citizen army defending the town. The Frenchmen, realizing that they were defeated and seeking to avoid a massacre, threw down their arms in surrender.

Marlon orders his men to cease firing, but in the heat of battle the soldiers disregard the command and continue shooting down the unarmed men. Marlon leaps out of the ditch, his arms outstretched, his face and neck swollen red with rage, and screams at the top of his voice, "Stop your firing! Why are you killing them? They are unarmed and have surrendered. Why are you murdering them?" Then he turns toward the fallen men with an expression of great remorse, as though to beg pardon for the tragic incident.

Edward Dmytryk, the director, shouted, "Cut! Print!" He was obviously delighted to see that Marlon intended to play his part at the top of his talent, not merely walk through the role in order to pay his debt to Zanuck, as he had done in playing Napoleon in *Desirée*.

I was disturbed, however, by something that seemed to be happening to Marlon while he was making this picture. Watching him, it seemed to me that he was no longer speaking as an actor, but rather he was declaiming to the world when he spoke his lines.

When he came off a scene he would say, "How was it, Freddie?" and one day I told him how I thought it was.

"You weren't talking to that other actor, then," I said. "You always say that if a message has to be slipped in, you've got to do it while you're entertaining. But now I see you talking right through the other actors to the audience. There was one line in that scene today—'You cannot remake the world from the basement of a dirty little police station'—and that's what you're trying to do."

The fact was that Marlon's commitment to social causes of various kinds was beginning to show in his acting. That was why he was "looking through" the others in the cast. Every line was a message, if it was possible to convey one, and this kind of self-indulgence was getting worse and worse. However praiseworthy his motives may have been, they were getting in the way of his art. Later, in *The Ugly American*, where there was mostly dialogue and very little action, he was expressing his political viewpoints more than he was acting, it seemed to me. Giving the messages, I thought, diminished his acting and made it weaker and less deep.

Back in Paris, something happened so unusual for Marlon

that it bears telling at length here. It's clear, I think, that he has little trouble getting a woman when he wants her. More often than not, in fact, it's the woman who casts a come-hither look at *him*. Quite often, women will confront him and offer themselves in any way that will please him. He is somewhat shy with beautiful women, but a direct, blunt approach really turns him on. He's always loved beautiful, brazen bitches.

Now and then, although it's relatively rare, some creature comes along who doesn't care at all for him in a sexual way. Even though it happens infrequently, it *has* happened, much to Marlon's consternation. His ego is hurt, his vanity wounded. His balloon bursts, and his desire for the cool, indifferent female increases tenfold. He must have her. In the years I've known him, he has come across several of these imperturbable darlings, and each experience has left him frustrated and flabbergasted.

In Paris, I met an extraordinarily sexy girl I'll call Corinne. I went into a small café on the Left Bank one day and saw her sitting alone on a high stool at the bar, sipping an aperitif. Except for the two of us and the bartender, the place was empty. Although it was late in the afternoon, the sun was still bright and hot, and the cool shade of the quiet café was invitingly tranquil.

I sat at a discreet distance from her and ordered a Pernod with ice and water. She kept her eyes lowered and I appraised her with an occasional sidelong glance. She was young, about nineteen, demure, and sensual. Her dark brown hair was becomingly close-cropped and she was extremely well groomed. The more I looked at her, the more attractive she seemed, and soon, without realizing it, I held her in a steady stare.

She must have felt my eyes on her because she raised her head, gave me a direct look, and smiled. I blushed, turned away quickly, and felt my blush deepening. I sipped my Pernod, composed myself, and thought, "She's a hooker, that's what she is, so what am I getting all shaky about?" There are few things that crush me as much as a rejection from a woman I really want. Knowing I can buy a woman removes the fear of rejection and gives me confidence. And I don't mind paying for a woman I desire.

She brought a cigarette to her lips and searched her bag for a match. I leaned toward her and held up a light for her. She thanked me in French. I spoke no French, and in English I asked to join her and buy her a drink. She smiled and promptly invited me to sit beside her, which I did. I was glad to find that she spoke English rather well. Eking out a conversation with awkward pantomime is enervating and makes a man less attractive. Prostitutes, especially when they like their client, enjoy communicating with him. It alleviates the uneasy knowledge that they can be bought for a price.

After some talk and several drinks, she said she was starving and wanted some dinner. I suggested a restaurant, and she gave a little cry of delight, saying that she knew the place and that it served excellent food. We stepped out to the street, hailed a taxi, and crossed the Seine to the Right Bank.

The weather was mild, and we sat outdoors at a table under a canopy. When the waiter came, she wondered if I would trust her to order dinner for both of us. Was I agreeable? Yes, I was agreeable. How could I refuse her? She ordered trout sautéed in sweet butter; boiled asparagus; plump peaches with a soft, ripe cheese; and a dry, white wine of rare vintage and very expensive.

It was a superb dinner, light yet satisfying, and easy to digest. When I was presented with the check, the enormous sum almost bowled me over, but I paid it with flair and left an extravagant tip, hoping I had enough cash left to pay the asking price for the charms of my precious darling.

It was still early in the evening, about seven-thirty, and I asked her where we could find some entertainment.

"Where is your hotel?" she asked.

"I'm staying at the Prince de Galles."

She gave me a little look of surprise and said, "But the Prince de Galles is directly across the street. We can see the entrance from here."

"I know," I said.

She laughed. "How convenient. Shall we go?"

We got up, crossed the street, entered the hotel, sailed through the lobby, and took the elevator to my room. Corinne was beautiful in bed. She was quickly and easily aroused. Mere kisses on her mouth and fondling of her breasts brought her to orgasm. And her orgasms were strong, full, and came one upon the other in rapid succession in an astonishing, numberless count. She moaned, whined, writhed, murmured, screamed, wept, laughed, bit, clawed, swooned, bucked, shouted obscenities, whispered endearments, babbled insanely, and on, and on, and on. My God, what a magnificent performance! When at last I had my orgasm, she went slack and slipped into a half-slumber with a smile on her lips. I looked at her and thought, Now here's someone who really loves her work.

Later that night, when she was in the bathroom and I had dressed to take her home, I placed some French francs on the dresser, a sum equivalent to about a hundred American dollars.

As we were about to leave, I said, "Don't forget to take your money."

"Take my . . ." She looked at me and giggled. "Do you think I am a . . . business woman?"

*Marlon and Barbara Rush as they
appeared in* The Young Lions.

Prostitutes in Paris sometimes describe themselves as "business women," pronouncing it "bizz-nazz woo-man."

"I don't know what to think," I said. "It all happened so quickly."

Corinne gave me a mischievous smile and said, "That is the way I am, when I am in the mood. Are you shocked?"

"A little," I said. "But mostly I'm happy and flattered."

"Of course, if I were poor, I would become a 'business woman.' And I would be a very good business woman. Because I would never, *never* go to bed with a man who did not make me ... hot? Is it the correct word? Hot?"

"Yes," I said, "that's exactly right."

"If I went to bed with a man who did not make me hot, then I think that I would . . . vomit? Is it correct? Vomit?"

"It's correct," I said.

"Do I speak good English?"

"Your English is excellent," I said.

She beamed with delight at the compliment and said, "Come, escort me home."

Arm in arm, we strolled down the deserted Avenue Foch.

"Do you desire to see me again?"

"Yes," I said.

"When? Tomorrow?"

"Yes. Tomorrow. Would you like to go to a dinner party?"

"Of course. I would like it very much."

"I'll pick you up at eight," I said, then hesitated and went on. "The host will be Marlon Brando."

"Marlon Brando? The actor?"

"Yes. I wasn't going to tell you. I wanted to surprise you."

"I'm glad you told me," she said. "I hate surprises of that kind."

"Do you like Marlon Brando?"

"Oh, yes! He is an exciting actor. And I hear that he is a very interesting man. Is it true, what they say, that he is . . . odd? That you never know what he will do? That he is . . ."

". . . unpredictable? Yes, it's true. But there are *times* when you know *exactly* what he will do."

I knew I was inviting disaster by introducing Corinne to Marlon. The moment he laid eyes on her, I knew he would immediately guide her to a bedroom and try to charm her out of her scented panties, leaving me alone to fume in humiliation. He had done it many times before, with girls not half as lovely as Corinne, and he would do it many times again, with girls we were yet to meet. The number of women who threw discretion to the winds for a tryst with Marlon was enough to make a cynic out of anyone, where love and fidelity were concerned.

When I picked up Corinne the following night, I was sure he would follow the scenario faithfully. She was wearing a semi-formal dress of black silk, simple but stylish, which did nothing to tone down or disguise the sensual contours of her body. She looked even lovelier, and sexier, than she had the night before, and I knew I could be sure that Marlon would zero in the moment he set eyes on her. For a moment I debated telling her that the dinner party had been canceled, so that I wouldn't lose her so soon after I'd found her. But I decided against it. I didn't want to hold a woman by hiding her or lying to her.

We arrived at Marlon's suite in the Hotel Raphael. I knocked on the door, and in a moment he appeared. When he saw Corinne, he smiled—not his genuine, spontaneous smile, but his practiced, charming, movie-star smile. He even kissed her hand and flattered her in French.

He asked us to come in, and when he had closed the door behind us, I turned and caught him throwing a swift, admiring glance at Corinne's shapely buttocks. It's beginning right on schedule, I thought.

The party was already in progress and picking up steam. Looking around the room, I saw Brigitte Bardot, Roger Vadim, and Marlon's best friend in France, Christian Marquand, the actor-director. After we had had an aperitif, I went to the buffet and fixed two plates of cold chicken cooked in wine, along with some small portions of tomato salad. I carried them out to the terrace and joined Corinne, who was lounging in a chaise and smoking a cigarette. We ate in silence, looking up at the dark, starry sky and the silhouettes of the city's rooftops. It was like the stage set for a hundred movies, most of them bad. I could almost see the title, "Paris —in the spring." Cynical though I might be, I had to admit that with the lovely Corinne half lying beside me, every line of her figure showing through her dress, springtime in Paris was just as romantic as all those lyricists and novelists had advertised it.

Marlon joined us, standing behind Corinne's chaise, and I could see that he was looking at and admiring what I had been contemplating. He bent over to whisper something in her ear. She smiled and shook her head. An expression of surprise and disappointment crossed Marlon's face, but, still smiling, he began to talk to her in French, which I couldn't understand. I didn't need a command of the language to know what he was saying, however. I knew him far too well for that. It was obvious that he was giving her his movie-star come-on, but to my surprise it was equally obvious that she was having none of it. He persisted, and still she demurred. He placed his hands on her shoulders and she shrugged them away, her frown plainly expressing her irritation with his persistence.

Then Marlon smiled and said rather stiffly in English that he was glad to have met her, and he hoped she was having a good time. He gave both of us a curt nod, walked away, and disappeared among his guests in the living room.

After a while, Corinne whispered that she wanted to be alone with me. As we walked back to the hotel, she looked up and remarked, "I thought you said Marlon was your friend."

"He *is* my friend," I said. "Why? What did he say to you?" I knew what the answer was going to be before she spoke.

"He asked me to go with him, to leave *you* and go with *him*."

"When did he ask you that?"

"On the terrace. Right in front of you. He asked, in

[220]

French, if I would go with him to the bedroom for a *tête-à-tête*."

"And what did you say?"

"I said that it was rude to speak French in the presence of someone who did not understand the language."

"In other words, you refused his invitation to go to the bedroom."

"Yes. There are many ways to say 'no' to a man without actually saying 'no.'"

"You resisted the temptation to go with him?"

"I felt no temptation to go with him. Not the slightest bit."

I was delighted, but I pretended to be surprised.

"Why not? He's handsome, rich, and famous. Only a few women have resisted the temptation, much less the invitation, to go with him. They are very rare, those women."

"Perhaps I did not go with him because I have too much pride."

"Pride?"

"Yes, I imagine he has many women waiting for him to call them. I have too much pride to be only one woman among many women. I want to be the only woman for a man. Even if it is just for a short time."

"Oh," I said, a little disappointed by her answer. I guess I wanted to hear her say that she had refused to go with Marlon because she had fallen in love with me.

Corinne glanced at me and smiled. "If you must know the truth, Carlo, it is this. As you say, Marlon is handsome, rich, and famous; but I have already told you—I would never, *never* go to bed with a man who did not make me hot. Marlon does not make me hot."

I was astonished and happy to hear it.

Next day when I saw Marlon at his hotel, the first thing

he said was, "Say, Freddie, that was some bitch you had last night at the party. I'd sure like a taste of that."

"I know you would," I said, "but I have to tell you, she's got no eyes for you, man."

"What do you mean, 'no eyes'? Why is she any different from the others? You can set it up for me."

"No, I won't do it."

"Come on, Freddie, do me a big favor. Set it up for me if you can. This chick is really solid."

"Well, don't depend on it."

"Is she as good a ball as she looks?"

"Better." I decided to lay it on as heavily as possible. "I started to count her orgasms last night, but I lost count at sixteen and had to stop."

As I expected it would, that made Marlon want her more than ever. He was always hung up on girls who had multiple orgasms, and the thought that this lovely, sexy girl had them, and had put him down when he tried to come on with her, drove him wild.

"I've just got to have that broad, Freddie," he said. "Now do me a *very* big favor and try to straighten me out with her."

We talked about other matters, and soon Marquand came in and joined us, along with another friend. After a while Corinne called up from the lobby. We went down and met her and began walking down one of the broad Parisian boulevards, five abreast, on our way to lunch. A building construction project suddenly narrowed the sidewalk and we had to split up. Corinne and I moved ahead and the others followed behind us. I was feeling very proud and happy to have Corinne on my arm, knowing how utterly charming she looked in her spring frock. I was also aware that Marlon, following behind, must be entranced with the movement of her trim buttocks. I wasn't surprised when he suddenly ran ahead to join us, but I was brutally shocked when he said abruptly in English, "Carlo told me you had sixteen orgasms last night. Is that true?"

Glancing at Corinne's face, I could see the sudden hurt in her eyes, to realize that I had talked about our intimacies to him. But she looked at him and then at me, and seeing the obvious shock and hurt I was feeling from the realization that Marlon would do such a thing to me, she suddenly seemed to make up her mind.

Putting her hand under my arm and squeezing it slightly, she said, looking squarely at Marlon, "Yes, it is true, and I often have even more—but only with Carlo."

Marlon looked flabbergasted. For once he couldn't think of anything to say and dropped back with the others.

As soon as Marlon and I were alone together later that day, I said, "What made you say something like that? How the hell could you do that to me, telling her something I'd told you in confidence. Are you crazy, man?"

He nodded his head. "Yes, I am, Freddie. Where women are concerned, I'm crazy. You ought to know that by this time. When I was walking behind you, watching her ass move, I couldn't resist, and I didn't even try."

"Well, whatever chance you might have had with Corinne, you ruined it."

That was the end of the episode, and there was never another one like it in our long relationship. I saw Corinne often until we had to leave Paris, when we broke it up, regretfully. I supposed we were almost, but not quite, in love.

CHAPTER SIXTEEN

WE WERE TO SHOOT the interiors for *The Young Lions* in Hollywood, but there were a few exteriors to do too, desert stuff, and they were to be filmed near the little town of Borrego Springs, in Southern California. The company took over the town's only motel, with its twenty cottages sprinkled about on the sand, and we went to work.

Almost immediately, Anna came to visit. She and Marlon were not yet married, but it was imminent and she wasn't letting him out of her sight any longer than possible. I had dinner with them the first night she was there, in the town's only restaurant, and after that we ate together nearly every night. This sociable behavior, which Marlon and I had enjoyed together for so long, roused Anna's ever-ready jealousy.

After dinner one night, when she was alone with Marlon, she told him she'd heard that I had offered to work for Logan, and she said it was clear to her that I was only using him, meaning Marlon, to further my own career. Next night, in her presence, he repeated the story.

"Is that true?" he asked me.

I sat there under her glaring eyes, my own face pale from the sheer impact of this viciousness. For a minute, I couldn't find the words to answer him.

"It must be true," Marlon said before I could say anything. "You're pale, and I can see you're very angry. And look there, your hand is shaking so you can't even hold your fork still."

"If I'm pale and angry and all that, it's because it's such a stupid lie," I said. "Where's your common sense? Why would I do anything as dumb as that? It would be like leaving a king to work for a courtier. You know what I think of Logan— we've talked about it often enough. He's a nice guy, but you know him as well as I do, and you know he isn't likely to listen to any of *my* shit."

"Okay, I believe you," Marlon said, and I could see he did. "It's probably just one of those stories that go around."

I wasn't so ready to pass it off. It didn't take much intuition to see that Anna was going to break up our friendship if she could. Next day, I tried again to warn Marlon against marrying her. "If you do," I said, "she'll fuck you up, that's for certain."

As I've said, I think he had the same premonition about her that I did, but the pregnancy hadn't occurred yet.

The day before we finished shooting the desert scenes, Anna drove up from Hollywood in her little white Ford to take Marlon home.

[225]

"Why don't you drive back with us?" Marlon invited me.

"No, man, thank you," I said, "not after those lies she told about me."

"Oh, come on, you'll make it up. I'll bet you'll wind up liking each other again."

I knew that wasn't going to happen, but I agreed to go along anyway—another mistake. As we began the drive back, the road led up from the desert over the mountains, along switchbacks that snaked up one side and would take us down the other side in the same twisting fashion, around one blind curve after another. Marlon was driving, but it wasn't long before Anna was begging him to let her get behind the wheel. She had just learned to drive, she said, and loved it.

Marlon didn't say yes or no, but when we stopped for coffee and came out again, there was a fast shuffle, and before I knew it Anna was in the driver's seat. She and Marlon sat in the front, and I climbed in behind.

It didn't take long for me to see that she was one of the worst drivers I had ever had the misfortune to share a car with. Not only was she mechanically inept, but she had a great deal of difficulty keeping her eyes on the road. Whenever she talked to you, she had to look at you, which I had seen her do at the dinner table and elsewhere, but it never occurred to me she'd do the same thing while she was driving a car on a mountain road.

Marlon was like Tennessee Williams' cat on a hot tin roof. "Watch that!" he'd yell from time to time, but Anna drove on, utterly oblivious of everything. Occasionally she would even turn around to say something to me, while both Marlon and I sat petrified until I simply lay down in the seat and closed my eyes. I couldn't look anymore.

"Why don't you pull over next chance you get, and I'll drive," Marlon said. "You're still kind of new at it."

"Oh, no," Anna said cheerfully, "I'm all right. And I'm having a wonderful time." She absolutely refused to give up the wheel.

We stopped for gas, and while Anna was in the rest room, I said to Marlon, "I'm not going to get back in that car again."

"But we're a long way from home," Marlon said.

"I don't care. I'll get there some way—alive. I like it better that way."

When Anna came out, Marlon said quickly, "I'll drive the rest of the way. We'll get home sooner."

"But I *must* drive," Anna said firmly.

"Why *must* you?" Marlon wanted to know.

"Because I get motion sickness very easily, and driving helps me to fight it off. I don't get sick when I drive."

While Marlon was trying to think of an answer for that one, she slid quickly behind the wheel again. There was no help for it; we had to go with her if we wanted to get home. I'd been brave about hitchhiking, but I knew I wasn't going to do that, not from this remote part of California. The last leg of the journey was the worst. To show us that she was relaxed, apparently, Anna took the curves in the wrong lane from time to time, while glancing over her shoulder to say something to me.

"You don't have to do that, Anna," I said pleadingly. "I'm listening to you. It's better to keep your eyes on the road."

We narrowly missed having an accident three or four times, and I could see Marlon watching Anna rather strangely. I thought he might be beginning to think that she was some kind of nut.

Later I said to him, "Look, do you need any more evidence that this girl is trouble? The lies, the jealousy all the time, and now this insane driving. Believe me, Marlon, it will only be the beginning."

As I've said, I know he was thinking it over when she got pregnant. About the same time, a big scandal arose over whether she was really Indian or whether she was Irish. There were explanations and denials, and it didn't really matter much anyway, except that it was clear to Marlon after a while that she had been lying about at least part of her past. I tried again, just after she announced she was pregnant.

"Let her have anything," I said to Marlon, "only don't marry her."

"But it's going to be my child too," Marlon said. And soon after, he married her.

After they were married, Marlon often used the excuse of having to see me so he could get away and have dates with other girls, but Anna figured that one out without much difficulty. Whenever she thought he was up to something, she would call me and everybody else she knew, trying to find him. Where Marlon was concerned, she seemed to have no pride whatever. If she was able to track him down somewhere, she would plead that she felt very ill and would he please come home immediately. Once, when this occurred, I happened to be with Marlon and went home with him. We found Anna on the floor in a state of hysteria, and it was very hard for Marlon to calm her down.

Another time, when Marlon called me to say he had a date with a girl, he asked me to say, if Anna called, that he had been with me and just left. I drew the line.

"No, I'm not going to be your beard this time," I said.

"What's the matter? Why not?" he wanted to know.

"Frankly, because I'm scared to death of that girl," I said.

I could see that she was getting angrier and angrier at Marlon and at me as well. I'd seen her at the height of one of her quarrels with my friend, and it was frightening. She came at you with her teeth bared, like a primitive woman. During one argument, she came out of the bathroom with a huge bar of soap in her hand and let it fly at Marlon. It got him between the eyes and cracked in half. Stunned, he staggered back and almost fell. Usually when she came at him, he just put up his arms and tucked his head in, but she hadn't given him the opportunity that time.

I remember only once when Marlon himself showed real anger toward her. It was after their little boy, Christian, was born. He adored the child, and I think it worried him that the boy spent so much time with Anna. He had taken a little one-room place on the unfashionable side of Wilshire Boulevard where the story conferences we were beginning to have about the Western could take place in privacy. In order to ensure that privacy, he didn't tell Anna where his hideout was, but with her relentless, jealous cunning, she tracked him down.

We were working there one afternoon when a knock sounded on the door, and when Marlon opened it, Anna burst in. Without any further preliminary, she began beating at him with her fists, in a frenzy of rage. But this time Marlon reached out, grabbed her, and held her in front of him like a doll.

"Where's Christian?" he demanded.

"I left him in the car, just down the street," Anna said defiantly but a little scared.

"*What?*" Marlon roared. He pushed her aside and ran out of the house in the direction Anna was pointing. The car was no more than a hundred yards away, but a movie star with a child can't take such chances, and in any case it would have been dangerous to leave an active little boy of that age alone in a car. Fortunately, he was sitting quietly, waiting for his mother to come back.

[229]

Anna Kashfi taking a swing at her ex-husband as they leave a courtroom after a custody fight. (WIDE WORLD PHOTOS)

Anna began taking pills and threatening suicide. She was on the defensive now, and Marlon was taking advantage of her. I was more afraid of her than ever and really believed, whether it was true or not, that she was quite capable of killing me if she was convinced that I stood between her and Marlon.

As everyone now knows, the marriage didn't last long, and the divorce proceedings, with the resulting custody fight, were a messy affair. The whole thing was a disaster, and Marlon was well out of it at last.

All this, you must understand, was only a distraction, although a major one, for Marlon. With all of his other commitments now out of the way, he was free at last to work on his Western, and it was rapidly becoming an obsession with him.

At this juncture he had reached a turning point in his life and career. His mother was dead, his father had failed in business, he had won an Oscar, and Paramount had given him carte blanche to make a picture his own way. Anna was at least relatively out of his life. They were separated, and she and Christian were living in the Brando home in Hollywood Hills. Marlon lived in what could almost be called a tract house—the one-bedroom place in an unfashionable neighborhood where Anna had eventually tracked him down.

For the Western, Marlon's first problem was to get a script, and he was reading various treatments that were being given to him by hopeful writers. He had quite a few people working for him by this time, including me, although it was an act of friendship, since I was on salary only when I was actually doing a job for him. But Stanley Kubrick was on his staff and a producer named Frank P. Rosenberg. He was very particular about that P. It set him off from the other Rosenbergs. All of these people were being paid but me, yet I was working too, reading scripts.

"Here," Marlon said, "read this one for me. It's by Liam O'Brien."

I read it and found the script an obviously tailored job, designed to conform with what the writer thought Marlon was like.

"Is there anything in it?" Marlon asked me later.

"Nothing," I said.

"But I paid him thirty-five thousand dollars to write it."

"Then you paid a thousand a page for nothing."

Sam Peckinpah produced a script that Marlon liked well enough to go into production until he changed his mind and paid off still another failure. Rod Serling, an old and experienced hand at this sort of thing, also failed to make it with Marlon. Then Calder Willingham, the novelist and screenwriter, produced something that seemed possible and Marlon asked me to read it. I balked at last.

"Listen," I said, "you're paying everyone else around here but me, and I'm reading all these scripts for nothing."

Marlon was instantly apologetic. "I never thought about that, Freddie," he said. "I'll pay your usual two hundred and fifty dollars a week."

"You're paying the others a lot more than that for doing a hell of a lot less work."

"Well, how much do you want?"

"Five hundred dollars."

"You mean you won't read for less than five hundred dollars?"

"That's what I mean."

"Okay, you've got it."

I read Willingham's script and thought he had given the thing a good, sound construction, but apparently Marlon had decided that this was going to be Calder's only contribution and he would have to go from the group that was toiling away at trying to put a movie together, in the hot confines of the little apartment, which Marlon had mistakenly thought would protect him from Anna and any other intruder.

I was now invited to be a member of this group, which included Frank P. Rosenberg, Kubrick, and Calder at that point. Kubrick protested my inclusion, although we had never met, which was ironic because *he* would not have been in the group if it hadn't been for me. That had come about when Marlon, trying to find a script, was also searching for a director, and I was helping him do it.

For weeks he pulled me around with him to see some of the lousiest American movies ever made. After we'd seen a particularly bad one, I said, "Why in hell did you drag me to see *this* movie? We knew it was a stinker. So why?"

"I'm looking for a director," Marlon said.

"But I thought *you* were going to direct."

"I've changed my mind. I've got too much to do as it is. And besides, Paramount might not stand still for it."

"What about Stanley Kubrick?"

"Who's he?"

"He's a film director."

"What's he done?"

"*The Killing* and *Paths of Glory*."

"Were they good?"

"They were better than good. They were brilliant."

"Okay. I'll call MCA and have them run them for us."

A few days later we were seated comfortably in a plush projection room at MCA in Beverly Hills. It was after dinner, and a kind of cocktail-party atmosphere prevailed. Several important agents were there with their wives. Two junior agents, boys in charcoal-gray suits, with white shirts and black knit ties, served drinks from the bar. They saw to it that my glass was never empty. I learned later that my suggestion to Marlon to consider Kubrick as the director for his Western was an especially happy one, because Kubrick was an MCA client. With Brando and Kubrick teamed, MCA would have quite a bit of control in the production of the film. The more clout the better, as they say in the agencies.

The lights were lowered, a wall rose slowly to reveal a screen, and *The Killing* was projected. I sat next to Marlon and observed him occasionally with sidelong glances. From beginning to end, he was enthralled by the fast-paced thriller.

The lights came up and everyone was looking at Marlon to see how the picture had affected him.

"How come I never even heard of this film?" he inquired, getting to his feet.

One of the agents said that the movie was a sleeper, that it hadn't had much publicity and wasn't exploited properly.

"Then why not buy the film and reissue it?" Marlon wanted to know.

"That's a good idea," the agent said, frowning to indicate he really didn't think so, "but we've got bigger fish to fry. Much bigger."

After a short intermission, we settled in our seats again to see *Paths of Glory.* Marlon was also much impressed with this war movie, and it was obvious to everyone that Kubrick had that night become a heavy favorite in the race.

For a couple of weeks after that I didn't hear from Marlon and I was puzzled. At last he called and said, "Why don't you ever call *me?* Why do I *always* have to call *you?*"

We had had this kind of talk several times before, and once again I repeated, "Because every time I've called you, you've been too busy to see me. So I figured that since you're the busy one, I'd wait until you were free to call *me.*"

"You sound just like a girl," Marlon said.

"*You're* the one that's like a girl. Whenever you're wanted, you back off. But when you're ignored, you start kicking down the door."

"That's a game girls play."

"Girls and movie stars."

"Man, you've got a bad mouth. Do you know why an Italian is called a wop? Because that's the sound shit makes when it hits the wall—*wop!*"

"Listen. I want you to hear this. Are you listening?"

"Yeah, I'm listening," Marlon said irritably.

I hung up quietly.

Almost immediately the phone rang. He was back on again, as though nothing had happened.

"Let's have dinner tonight. I'll drive by and pick you up. At eight." Before I could answer, *he* hung up.

We had dinner at a Mexican joint downtown. The food was fair, but the waitress had an ass that wouldn't quit. She was a sultry, dark-eyed seventeen-year-old, and when she walked you could have ground coffee in the movement of her buttocks.

Whenever she passed, Marlon gazed with awe at her rear. "Man, dig those buns!" he kept saying.

She would stop at the table every now and then, and Marlon would practice his Spanish, flirting with her. All the Mexicans, especially the men, smiled in approval at this love play. Marlon Brando was *mucho hombre* and showed a proper appreciation for a fine-looking woman.

"What have you been doing?" I asked.

"Oh, nothing much. Just seeing a buddy of mine." He tossed it off in a way that aroused my curiosity.

"Who?"

"Stanley Kubrick. Do you know him?"

"Do I know him! I'm the guy who brought him to your attention. Remember?"

"Oh, yeah, that's right. Well, I've decided on him to direct the Western."

"Great!"

"Hold it," Marlon said. "He doesn't want *you* on the picture."

"Why not? He doesn't know me. We've never met."

"I know, but he's heard about you. Somebody's told him that I listen to you more than I listen to directors, and when he's working he doesn't want any other directors around. He doesn't want you on the set."

"Does Kubrick know I got him the job?"

"No. And listen—don't spread that around. I want him to think that I thought of him—that *I* wanted him. It makes for a better relationship between actor and director. Okay?"

"Okay," I said. "But now what?"

"Don't worry. You'll work with me. Let me handle it."

"But Stanley's the director, and if he—"

"This is *my* picture. My toy. And nobody's going to tell me who works in it and who doesn't. Nobody. I'm The Man."

"But it's a hell of a way to start working on a movie. You need a team. Guys helping each other. Not against one another."

"Don't worry. Things'll work out. Let me handle it. Okay?"

"All right," I said.

My first meeting with Kubrick was wary. Marlon had cautioned me only to observe. "Keep your mouth shut for the first few meetings" was the way he put it. Then he explained what he was going to do. He intended to fire Willingham, whom Kubrick had brought in as scenarist, and after that happened I would be brought into the conference as a regular member.

As I watched all these important people talking together at the first conference, I thought they behaved like small boys. There was a lot of rhetoric, a little sense, but mostly bullshit. Kubrick gave an impression of brilliance, but it seemed to me he was more money-hungry than anything else. It also appeared that he had no idea of character, which may explain his later hangup on science fiction. Willingham looked defeated. Whenever he raised his voice, it seemed, he was turned down. Sensing that he wasn't going to last long, he got very nervous and began writing under every line of his dialogue a parenthetical note about what it really meant.

Obviously, he was going to go, but in true Hollywood fashion, Willingham was the last to be sure of it. Marlon did the firing in his own inimitable fashion. He took Willingham out for a night on the town, gave him a good dinner, and by the time he had finished his lamb chops, he was fired. As a parting gift, Marlon gave him an expensive inlaid rosewood chess table.

Now I was in the conference and had my vote. I was sure that Kubrick was going to be the next to go, and I watched him while ideas were being bandied about. He was always in motion, running his fingers through his hair, doodling on a pad, or diddling a loose bridge or shaky tooth at the back of his mouth. It was strange to see his New York pallor among the perpetual suntans of Hollywood; the Californians, synthetic and real, observed that his body had gone too long without exercise.

He and Marlon were often at odds. Marlon, for example, wanted Karl Malden to play Dad Longworth, the antagonist in the picture, but Kubrick thought Malden was wrong for the part, and so did I. To convince Marlon of that, however, would take some doing. Dad Longworth, as his name suggested, was Marlon's "father figure" in the movie, and at the climax "father and son" had a violent showdown.

"I don't think Karl Malden would be effective in the part," Kubrick said.

"Why not?" Marlon protested. "Karl's a good actor."

"Yes, he is, but there's something else to be considered."

"What's that?"

"There's a contest between you and Dad, conflict between good and evil. We flash your face on the screen and we see a winner. Flash Karl Malden's face on the screen and we see an actor who usually plays losers. So there's no contest. We need a stronger actor to play against you; we need a winner. Let's put two champions in the arena."

"And whom do you suggest?" Marlon wanted to know.

"Spencer Tracy."

"I promised Karl the part a long time ago. And he's been waiting for it, refusing other parts."

"Let's pay Malden his full salary, then. I wouldn't want him to lose any money."

"And that's it? Just pay him off?" Marlon said. "What will you tell him?"

"Tell him the truth. The script has been changed, and the part's not right for him now. When he hears we want Tracy, I'm sure he'll understand."

"I don't know," Marlon said doubtfully. "And anyway, Tracy might not want the part."

"The only way to find out is to ask him," Kubrick said.

Marlon paced back and forth, seemingly unable to reach a decision. He stopped, turned to me and said. "What do you think, Freddie?"

"I'll have to go with Stanley," I said. "I think Spencer Tracy would be perfect. With him in it, we're halfway home."

Marlon thought about it some more. Then he laughed and said, "I'm sorry, fellers, but the final decision is mine. Tracy is a fine actor, but I mean to keep my promise to Karl. He gets the part, so let's think along those lines. I don't want to hear anything more about it."

And that was that. The incident demonstrated something else, however. Marlon had thought I might "yes" him to death when I joined the conference, but it hadn't happened, and he was annoyed because I often sided with Kubrick. When there was an impasse, we took a vote and quite often, it seemed, Kubrick and I were voting against Marlon and Frank P. Rosenberg.

Yet Kubrick and I were hardly buddies underneath this surface agreement. He left his doodles behind one day, and glancing at them as I left the table, I saw that he had written,

"Carlo is a bright guy, but he wastes a lot of time." I was sure he had left his scratch-pad sheets behind deliberately so I would see them.

After a meeting one day we went for a stroll and had a little talk.

"Do you know of Henri Cartier-Bresson?" Kubrick inquired.

"Yes," I said, "he's a French photographer. An artist. I've seen his pictures in magazines and in museums."

"That's the guy," Kubrick said. "Well, I suggested using Cartier-Bresson as the still photographer for the movie. I explained to Marlon that Bresson would accept the assignment because of the opportunity to work with him. His photographs are published all over the world. Just think of all that publicity, high-level stuff, Cartier-Bresson on Brando. That kind of publicity is priceless. And it's all free. Can you imagine anything better?"

"What did Marlon say?"

"He rejected it."

"Why?"

"I don't know. He said he'd think about it. But I think he's going to let the suggestion die—a pocket veto."

Some time later I asked Marlon why he'd rejected the idea. "I want to feel free to tell a still photographer to split when I don't want to be photographed," he said. "I can't order an artist like Cartier-Bresson to stop snapping his shutter at me and get lost. It wouldn't be nice."

"My dear friend," I said, "intelligent and talented as you are, sometimes you're a jackass."

He was also the boss, and Kubrick was about to understand that fact. Our story conferences were becoming stormier. Sometimes we were all shouting at once at the top of our

The author, Frank P. Rosenberg, and Guy Trosper.

voices, and Marlon would strike a Japanese gong with a mallet to silence us. I was helping Marlon rewrite Willingham's script, and it went from bad to worse.

Finally another writer was called in, Guy Trosper, an "old pro" who struck up an immediate rapport with Marlon. Poor Guy, who was a nice chap, unfortunately gave off a peculiar body odor, a sweet, sickly smell. He himself was not aware of it, but I certainly was, since I shared an office with him and shared a secretary as well. She and another secretary were having lunch one day when Trosper came in to work, and when I got there a little later I found them in an outer room, crying. They were embarrassed and reluctant to tell me why at first, but then they confessed Trosper had removed his jacket, at which the odor had become so overwhelming that it filled the office and ruined their lunch. I told Marlon about it, and without mincing any words he advised Guy to use a deodorant because there had been complaints. Trosper's own embarrassment must have been acute, but from then on he was deodorized.

Quite often Kubrick found himself in disagreement with Trosper, and we all quarreled over each small point of difference, interminably. After a particularly bad session, it was decided (by all of us except Kubrick, who wasn't there) that Stanley would have to go. Two geniuses on one picture was one genius too many.

Marlon always pretends to be going through an agonizing decision when he is going to fire someone, but I notice he always manages to have several witnesses around when he does it. He also plays a whole bullshit scene around the idea of "How can I do it to him without causing him pain?" Then he does it in the worst possible way. The point of the whole exercise is that he doesn't want anyone to think that someone could possibly leave him.

I wasn't surprised that he had decided to fire Kubrick. He had always intended to direct, I was sure. Certainly he'd talked about it often enough. I was sure that he knew all along what he was doing and that he'd simply gotten everybody involved with the picture worked up to a certain point and was only waiting for the proper time, which was now.

But then he said to me, inexplicably, "Listen, Freddie, see if you can find out from Kubrick how he'd feel if he was fired."

"I know damn well how he'd feel, and so do you," I said.

"Okay, but try to find out anyway."

We had dinner soon after, Kubrick and I, and I got around to asking him indirectly, or as indirectly as I could. Kubrick looked surprised but not alarmed; I don't think it occurred to him that such a thing could happen to him at this point.

"Why, I don't know, Carlo," he said thoughtfully, answering my question. "I guess I'd survive. I always have."

Nevertheless, he was stunned when it happened. A meeting was arranged at MCA, and Kubrick, unaware of the purpose of the session, was informed that he was off the picture; they had decided to find someone else. Stanley was so dumfounded he could say nothing, and the silence stretched out into an embarrassed eternity, which Marlon broke.

"This is like being in a room with a ten-foot kangaroo," he said. "Come on, let's get out of here."

Many directors were considered, but Marlon rejected them all until the magic moment when he suggested, "What about *my* directing it?"

The suggestion set bells ringing and doves flying in Frank P. Rosenberg's belfry. "Are you serious? Do you really want to direct it?" he asked Marlon.

"Mmmmm—yeah," Marlon admitted. "I'd like to take a whack at it."

"I'll bring it over to Paramount and see how they feel about it," Frank P. Rosenberg promised. "I don't think they'll give us any trouble."

To no one's surprise, Paramount gave Marlon his first directorial assignment a couple of days later.

Soon after, I was having dinner one night at Kubrick's home. He was still in a funk about his dismissal.

"Has Marlon found a director?" he asked.

"Yeah," I said.

"Who?"

"Marlon's going to direct it."

Kubrick's depression lifted immediately.

"You seem relieved," I said.

"I *am* relieved. If he had hired another director, it might have appeared that I was lacking in talent, or temperament, or something. But if Marlon directs it, it gets me off the hook."

"Maybe you're right," I said. "I didn't think of it that way."

"And I can see Marlon's point. You can't really call a film your own if someone else directs it."

"Still—I'm sorry to see you go."

"Thanks. You must know that Marlon depends on you quite a bit. Well, he'll really need a friend now. Don't let him down."

"I'll try not to," I said.

Our entourage now included George Glass and Walter Seltzer, who had been hired by Marlon to be executive producer. Seltzer was a nice chap, quiet and unassuming; but Glass, who had been Kramer's publicity man, was a pushy little fellow, about five feet four, a real Hollywood type who elbowed his way along, interrupting, hustling, always hungry.

"Look, Carlo," he said to me one day, "I've got a great title for the picture."

"That's good," I said. "Nobody's thought of a decent one yet."

"Yeah, yeah, that's right. Well, how do you like this— *Guns Up. Guns Up.* Get it? Get the symbolism?"

"What?"

"Like a hard-on, see, Carlo?"

When I passed this magnificent idea to Marlon, he said, "I'm just keeping George quiet. Tell him anything you can think of. But I'll think of a title."

And he did. *Burst of Vermilion* had long since been abandoned. Marlon realized he would have to do better than that,

Marlon and his unknown leading lady in One-Eyed Jacks, *Pina Pellicer.* (WIDE WORLD PHOTOS)

so eventually he came up with *One-Eyed Jacks*. It had two meanings, he pointed out to me. In playing cards, only two jacks have a single eye, and some poker players play these cards wild. So too, said Marlon, some men show only one side of themselves, and they're wild. I wasn't crazy about this one either, but it was considerably better than *Guns Up*, to put it conservatively.

Now we were ready for the casting. I tried to convince Marlon he should persuade Dolores Del Rio to come out of retirement and play one of the parts, but he was set on Katy Jurado. Marlon thought Del Rio was too aristocratic and too old, but it seemed to me she looked younger than Jurado.

The leading lady hadn't been cast yet, and Frank P. Rosenberg went to Mexico City to find an actress. Before he left, Marlon told him, "No tits. I don't want my leading lady heaving big boobs on that wide screen while I'm trying to get an important point across to my audience."

After this briefing, Frank P. Rosenberg went to Mexico City, set up an office, and began to interview actresses on camera. One of those who came in was an actress named Pina Pellicer, and when her filmed interview reached Marlon, he liked it best. When she appeared in his office, it was clear that Frank P. Rosenberg had followed the boss's instructions to the letter—or to the tit. Pina was absolutely flat, a washboard, a breastplate. She had been playing a Spanish-language version of *The Diary of Anne Frank* in Mexico, and something of that poor girl's terrible tension appeared to be within her. She was like an exposed nerve, thin, frightened, and full of a kind of anger. Consequently it was difficult to feel sorry for her, and since she listened only to Marlon, no one else could be friendly with her. She committed suicide some time after the picture was finished.

Marlon did much of the interviewing himself, and his

technique was direct. Searching for an actress whose emotions he could control, he was interviewing a girl named Nina Martinez one day, a very sexy female who in time became the playmate of the entire cast. Before she was signed, she came in for an interview at which we were all present.

"Have you ever had a producer ask you to raise your skirt?" Marlon asked her abruptly.

"Yes," she admitted, with candid calm.

"Who?" Marlon demanded.

She pointed to Frank P. Rosenberg, who looked taken aback for once.

"Are you a virgin?" Marlon asked.

"No." Matter-of-factly.

"Do you have a family back home?"

"Yes, I do," and she named them.

"Who's your favorite person in the family?"

She named an eight-year-old niece.

Then Marlon made up the most horrible story he could think of about the niece, how she had been involved in a tragic accident, hit by a truck, and her broken, shattered body scattered across the road. As he talked, Martinez began to cry and soon became nearly hysterical.

Marlon was satisfied. "Okay," he said, "you got the part."

That was how he cast, and he would use the same technique on the set to get the effects he wanted from actors. As an actor himself, he could do persuasive, wonderful things with his voice—unlike people like Frank P. Rosenberg, whose very tone could set your teeth on edge. When Kubrick was going to be fired, for instance, and everyone knew it but him, the atmosphere in the conference changed toward him, and suddenly everyone was disrespectful. You could hear it in their voices. Frank P. Rosenberg was easily the nastiest, because he was currying favor with Marlon and now it was safe to show Kubrick how powerful he was, and he did it by riding him in his strident voice at the story conferences. Kubrick, who couldn't understand why everyone was treating him this way, complained about it. There was an argument, and Frank P. Rosenberg threatened to throw him out of the window.

"You're bigger and stronger than I am," Kubrick said, "so if you want to fight, do you mind if I pick somebody to stand in for me, someone like Tim Carey?" Carey was a muscular, powerful man who played the villain in the picture.

Marlon broke it up. He advised Frank P. Rosenberg to cool it.

By this time two years had gone by and about a half million dollars spent in trying to develop a satisfactory screenplay and get the movie into production. Paramount finally set a shooting date; and the scenes were outlined enough to set the technicians to work. Marlon worked frantically, overseeing everything down to the smallest detail—casting, costumes, set designs, locations. If nothing else, his Western would be beautifully mounted.

Now we were ready to begin.

CHAPTER SEVENTEEN

O N THE FIRST day of shooting, Marlon, in costume, walked toward the camera and crew on the outdoor set. I was beside him. As we walked, I asked, "Are you nervous?"

He thought a little, smiled, and said, "You won't believe this. I thought I would be, but I'm not. Not at all. Are you?"

"No," I said. "But I'll bet the guys at Paramount are holding their breath."

Marlon broke up. "I'll bet they're shitting in their pants."

So after all the work and worry, we found the Big Moment not in the least thrilling or frightening. It was just the beginning of another long job of work. The excitement came later.

I never saw Marlon have so much fun, and it was contagious. Everyone felt it. For me, it was like being an overgrown kid playing cowboys-and-Indians.

After the first day's shooting, I drove back to the motel with Frank P. Rosenberg. We were silent, gazing at the marvelous vistas of Big Sur and the Pacific Ocean. Frank P. Rosenberg, who was driving, seemed glum. He stared straight ahead at the road, oblivious of the splendid, panoramic view.

To make conversation, I said, "I wonder why they call this part of the country Big Sur?"

"They should call it Big Tsouris," Frank P. Rosenberg harrumphed. (As even some Gentiles know, "tsouris" means "trouble" in Yiddish.)

"Something wrong?" I asked.

"Would you believe," he said, "that on the first day's shooting, we're five days behind schedule?"

"How can that be?" I said. "It sounds impossible."

He handed me three pages of script and asked me to examine them, which I did.

"We were scheduled to shoot those three pages today," he said. "How much did we actually get on film?"

I glanced at the pages again. "We got a half page. Only a half page?"

"That's all. A half page. If we go on at that rate, you can figure, as of now, that we're five days behind schedule."

"Wow!" I said.

"Wow is right," Frank P. Rosenberg said.

I've read a good many stories about Marlon's moodiness, his maddening search for the precise meaning of a scene, his frustrating demands for perfection, and his tendency to sulk when he doesn't get his way. Most of these tales are believed to be true because they fit in with the legend that Brando has become, but in fact they are mostly apocryphal.

[249]

I could see how some of them, at least, got started as the filming of *One-Eyed Jacks* went forward. We had several visitors from Hollywood—columnists, screen-magazine writers, reporters. They watched Marlon photographing the Pacific Ocean. For hours he scanned the sea for a wave to roll in and break just so, waiting for the perfect wave, not caring about the time and money expended.

That's what they said, but it was nonsense. The truth was that the weather had changed from the day before, and since he was shooting the same scene, the weather had to match. When a scene is put together in the cutting room, you can't have a clear, bright sky in one second and in the next a dull, cloudy sky—not, that is, if you want to keep on working in the movie business.

Charles Lang, the cinematographer, had called the weather bureau and was informed that the sun would soon dispel the clouds and the sea would calm. Instead of waiting for the mist to evaporate and the rough surf to abate, Marlon tried to get a dramatic shot of a wave as it hit a huge rock near the shore and shot a high, white plume in the air. Perhaps he could use it as an insert to punctuate or highlight a moment in the film. As it turned out, however, he found no use for the shot and it was discarded. But there was no time or money wasted; the crew would have had to be paid whether they were working or just standing around waiting for the weather to clear.

When the story reached Marlon that he had wasted thousands of dollars photographing waves, he shrugged his shoulders and remarked, "I've learned that it's useless to try to suppress stories like that. I don't even bother to deny them. People will believe what they want to believe."

Even while a film is in the making, the script is being constantly rewritten. At night, after dinner, we all gathered in Marlon's rooms and plotted the next day's setups. So far, the

daily rushes looked good. The movie had the vast, open look of a Western. But the original concept of intermingling good and evil in the characters, so that the hero and villain became indistinguishable, had gotten lost in the script changes. Consequently the picture was becoming the familiar, classical Western—a superficial, simple-minded melodrama of "good guys against the bad guys." Some time later Marlon was quoted as saying, "With this film I intend to storm the citadel of clichés." He was doing it, too.

As an actor in the picture, he was anything but a cliché, doing his usual serious, incredibly talented work. Only once did he overdo getting into the role, and that, oddly enough, was in the drunk scene. Such scenes were always hard for him because he somehow couldn't play a serious drunk with any kind of conviction. If he had to be one, in a movie or on the stage, he had actually to drink himself into that condition and then play against it, as most drinkers in fact do in life. Naturally, drinking scenes were always scheduled for the last shot of the day.

I had seen him play a drunk scene in *The Young Lions* with May Britt. Before he went on, he opened a quart of gin in his dressing room, gulped down several swallows, and waited for the effect. Then he went on drinking until he felt drunk enough to meet the scene's requirements.

In *One-Eyed Jacks*, he had to play a staggering, falling-down drunk. Just before the last shot of the day, we went to his dressing room and he began slugging away at a bottle of gin. He was drinking much too quickly, not waiting to determine the alcohol's effect. It was nearing six, quitting time, and he wanted to get the scene in the can before then, in order to avoid overtime payments. In no time, he had demolished almost half the bottle and he was still sober. As an experi-

Marlon, drunk, playing a drunk, with May Britt, receiving dialogue coaching from the author.

enced drinker, I warned him, "Wait a while. Don't drink any more. I think you've had enough."

"I've got to do a Leon Errol stagger in this scene, but I'm sober enough to walk a tightrope," he said, and went on slugging away.

I took the bottle from him. He had killed more than half of it, and I held it up to show him.

"Are you crazy?" I said. "Drinking like that can kill you."

"But I'm not drunk yet," Marlon protested.

"You will be. I'll give you ten to one you can't make it from here to the set. Ten bucks to one. Bet?"

"It's a bet."

It was about thirty paces from the the dressing room to the set. Marlon had negotiated about half the distance when his knees buckled. I grabbed him under the arm and pulled him up straight.

"I'm okay," he said.

"You're plastered."

Marlon giggled. "Man, I'm bombed."

[253]

He pitched forward but remained upright, miraculously. By the time he was in place to make his entrance, he could hardly stand without support. He leaned against the door he was to open and gave the signal for "Action." Camera and sound rolled, and Marlon slammed the door open. He staggered across the room, his eyes glazed and crossed, then he fell, pole-axed, on his face.

Some of us lifted and carried his dead weight back to the dressing room and stretched him out on the sofa. It was just six o'clock and the crew and actors were dismissed. A few people hung around to see if he was all right, but it was apparent he would be out for hours, and in a short time everyone went home.

There is nothing quite so desolate and depressing as a dark, empty movie set. The lighting equipment, camera, and props stand in the gloom like grotesque creatures that have died in their tracks. The only light was in Marlon's dressing room. I tried to read, but it was impossible for me to concentrate. A doctor finally came and examined the fallen star. "He's all right," the doctor delivered his verdict. "Keep an eye on him." Then he left.

Marlon, still out, began to throw up, and I held his head over the edge of the sofa so that he wouldn't strangle on his vomit as poor Tommy Dorsey had done. After he had emptied his stomach, I made him as comfortable as I could and cleaned up.

It was two o'clock in the morning when Marlon came to. "Wha' happened?" he muttered. "Where's everybody?"

"Everybody's gone home," I said. "It's two A.M."

Marlon raised himself on his elbows, then fell back again. "What hit me?" he wanted to know.

"The floor hit you," I said. "Do you think you can manage to walk to the car? There's a driver waiting to take you home."

"Don't leave me, Freddie. Don't leave me."

"I won't leave you until I see you home and safe in bed."

"You're my only friend, Freddie. My only friend. Everybody left but you. You stayed. I'll never forget it, Freddie. Never."

"Marlon, would you do me a favor?"

"Sure. Sure. Name it."

"Will you try to make it to the car? On the ride home you can stretch out and sleep. Okay?"

"Is that all? Sure. Sure."

He got to his feet and the driver and I, each holding an arm, half carried him to the car. All the way home he hung his head out the window to catch the breeze. By the time we arrived, he had sobered a little but was still wobbly. He felt like vomiting again, and I hurried him to the bathroom. He sprawled on the tile floor, held his chin over the edge of the toilet bowl, and threw up. He put his arms around the bowl and began to bawl like an infant. "This reminds me of my mother," he said. "I don't know why, but it reminds me of Mom."

He was still in costume and his stale makeup was smeared. He looked like a rodeo clown who had taken some severe bumps.

"I should shower, but the hell with it," he said. "I'll fall out this way. You go home and get some sleep."

"You'd better undress and get in the shower," I said. "You'll feel better for it in the morning."

He undressed, showered, shampooed, and brushed his teeth. He looked a hell of a lot better and he was almost completely sober.

"Thanks a lot, Freddie. I'll be all right now. It must be four o'clock. Go home and get some sleep. And don't come in before noon. Hear?"

[255]

"I hear," I said. "Are you taking the morning off?"

"Hell, no. I've had more than eight hours' sleep already. I'm ready to go to work now. But I'll nod out for a couple, three hours. See you later."

"Later," I said and left.

As the picture moved along, after this brief interruption, Marlon's enthusiasm for it increased every day. I had learned not to discuss my differences about the execution of a scene with him, at least not on the set. Although nothing was said to me, the assistant director and the executives from Paramount frowned at my long conferences with Marlon. I was wasting time, they thought, and time was money, and money was going down the drain. The picture had been budgeted at two and a half million, but now the cost of production was nearing six million. Before the studio could recoup its money and begin to show a profit, the movie would have to bring in twelve million dollars or more at the box office.

"What the hell is Marlon doing?" one of the Paramount executives complained bitterly. "Is he building a monument to himself? Will the shooting on this picture never end?"

Well, what the hell *was* Marlon doing? He was doing things like these.

Trying to work with the tense and nervous Pina Pellicer, for one thing. Here she was, playing in a Western, but she had never been on a horse. Every time she mounted, she plopped into the saddle like a hunk of hamburger. Worse than that, however, to get a simple reaction from her was frustratingly difficult.

In one scene at a dinner table she was so nervous that when the cameras began to roll the resulting footage was a disaster. Marlon stopped the scene and whispered some instructions to the cameramen. "Listen," he said, "we're going to shoot this next take, but we're not going to tell her we're doing it. When you start rolling, I want the rest of the crew to move as though you were getting ready to take the shot. But no noise. And I'll give you the signal when to roll." Then he started Pina in the scene again, as though it were a rehearsal, surreptitiously giving the signal to the cameramen. She was fooled and relaxed enough to finish the scene. But it had taken a whole reel of film to get a few seconds of reaction from her, and in the end it was snipped out. That kind of moviemaking is very expensive.

In another scene she was seen returning from the beach after being seduced there and slinking to her room along a wall. She put her hand around the corner and it touched a villain, Slim Pickens. Naturally, she was supposed to register fright, but her expression was so contrived that Marlon couldn't use it. He asked the prop man to bring him the loudest six-shooter he had and warned the camera crew to shoot without sound; it could be dubbed in later.

The scene was started again. As Pina's hand reached around the corner and touched Slim, Marlon fired the gun. He got the genuine reaction he was looking for, but a good actress would have done it in a few takes and we would have saved about $40,000.

It was that kind of struggle with poor Pina, from the beginning. On the first day of shooting, she had been so nervous that she had facial tics, and she appeared to be having trouble walking, taking the steps from place to place that were required. "My God, Marlon," I said, "she doesn't know enough to put her feet together when she stops." Yet both he and I tried to make her think she was great to bolster up what minute bit of confidence she possessed.

We had to give her riding lessons, of course, because even to show her mounting a horse, much less riding, was to demonstrate an exercise in awkwardness. It was a hell of a price to pay, I thought, just so Marlon could have a leading lady with no tits. And it wasn't that picture alone. In later years, when he had the power of cast selection, he never chose a really good-looking girl as his lead.

Another costly piece of business was teaching Larry Duran how to act. Duran, now a stunt man, was Marlon's stand-in. He was a reformed pickpocket who had never acted, yet Marlon had put him in the role of Modesto, his best friend in the picture.

There was a scene in which Ben Johnson was to call Duran a greaser, trying to goad him into a gunfight, but when Duran pulled out his gun and fired, it was empty. Ben Johnson had taken the bullets out.

"This what you looking for, greaser?" Ben was to say, throwing six shells into the air, at which Duran was supposed to register shock. It seemed to be beyond him. After several futile tries, there was a hurried conference and Marlon said, finally, "Okay, let's get on with it. We'll put him on a fake horse in an interior and get the reaction then." But when we came to it again in the shooting schedule, we wasted a whole morning and Duran still couldn't get it.

Once more Marlon resorted to his ruse with the camera crew. They were instructed to get close to Duran, to make certain the sound was all right, and to be sure that there was nothing wrong with the take in a technical sense.

"I'm going to do something," Marlon told them. "When I go up to him and start talking, you start rolling."

Marlon moved up to where Duran was sitting on a wooden horse, as the camera dollied in close.

"Larry," he said confidentially, "I want to tell you something."

Duran leaned over to hear, and as he did, Marlon gave him a haymaker of a slap on the face. That was his plan to get the proper shock reaction, and it would have worked except that he hadn't figured on the beard the makeup people had pasted on Duran. As Marlon's hand came away, part of the beard came with it, so it was hanging precariously on the actor's shocked face. He was shocked twice.

"Cut! Forget it," Marlon said disgustedly. "We'll just have to make do."

This was the kind of thing—all the incidents I've been describing here—that were sending the production costs soaring and elevating the blood pressure of Paramount's executives.

There were also little time-consuming arguments on the set, most of them trivial. For example, in one scene a gallows is being built to hang Marlon, and he's in jail listening to them building it when Pina comes to visit him. In the dialogue that follows, Marlon improvised a line. "I'll be thinking about you all the way," he says. It grated on my ear as I visualized Marlon thinking of her all the way from the top to the bottom of the gallows.

"That doesn't sound like a very good line," I said to him. " 'All the way' doesn't sound right."

"It'll work," Marlon assured me.

Just then Frank P. Rosenberg came over and began to complain about the same line. Instantly, Marlon's paranoia took over.

"Did you and Frank talk about this line?" he demanded suspiciously.

"Of course not," I said. "The fact that we're both complaining just proves the line is bad. We weren't in cahoots, believe me."

In the end, Marlon cut the line.

Occasionally, he was deliberately sloppy about details. In one scene, Malden says, "This will end your gunfighting days," and he brings his rifle down on Marlon's hand. Subsequently, Marlon appeared in the following scenes with his fingers stiff to show what had happened to him in recovering from the attack. Malden demurred. "With that kind of injury," he pointed out, "your fingers wouldn't be stiff, they would just hang limp, with no control."

But Marlon didn't care about any technicalities. He went for the drama and the hell with the rest.

CHAPTER EIGHTEEN

I WAS BROWSING in a second hand bookstore on an off day when I found an early novel by Vladimir Nabokov called *Laughter in the Dark*. It was a paperback, much used, dog-eared, and coming apart. Nabokov had just published *Lolita*, it had risen quickly on the bestseller lists, and Kubrick and his partner, Jim Harris, had bought the movie rights for a price in six figures.

Out of curiosity, I bought *Laughter in the Dark* for fifteen cents. I went home and read it at once, finding it to be a finger exercise for *Lolita*, except that Margot, the girl in *Laughter*, was a few years older. It was a brilliant black comedy, and I thought it would make an excellent movie.

With my agent, Richard Wookey, I went to see Irving "Swifty" Lazar, who was representing Nabokov on the West Coast. I made him an offer for the movie rights to *Laughter*, and Lazar said he would consider it. He got some competitive bidding going and a little later told me I could have the book if I met the top bid. The going price was far more than I could afford, but obviously the property was now "hot" and I went immediately to Kubrick, afraid some shrewd producer might get hold of it, make a "quickie," and cash in on the *Lolita* publicity.

Kubrick was astonished when I showed him this early Nabokov novel. No one seemed to know such a book existed. "Are you trying to hustle me?" he asked bluntly. "Or do you really believe this novel will make a good movie?"

"You know better than that," I said. "You could lift the story, as it is, right out of the book and put it on film. It'll make an excellent movie. Read it."

About a week later, I was invited to Malibu to have dinner with Kubrick and Harris, who told me, "We've decided to buy *Laughter in the Dark* for two reasons. One, we don't want anybody else to have it, not before we make *Lolita*. It's insurance, so to speak. Two, we also think it'll make a good movie. Now—how would you like to do the screenplay?"

"I'd like that very much," I said.

Harris made an offer and I accepted.

"You've got lots of time," Kubrick said. "We'll draw up the contracts and you can start on *Laughter* when you're through with *One-Eyed Jacks*. I'll be busy with *Spartacus* for quite a while, so, as I said, you've got lots of time."

But then, not long after that conversation, I had another offer.

"Right after *One-Eyed Jacks*," Marlon said, "I'm going to New York to do *The Fugitive Kind*. Coming with me?"

"I've got a deal going with Kubrick and Harris," I told him. "I haven't signed with them yet, so I won't know anything for certain until I do."

"When will you know?"

"I'll know in a week," I said. "But let's figure on ten days, just to be sure."

"Okay," Marlon said. "Ten days. But let me know sooner if you can. They're bugging me to sign, and I can't stall them much longer."

Ten days later I was with Marlon while he was undressing to take a shower.

"Your ten days are up," he said. "Are you coming with me, or are you going with Kubrick?"

"I've just signed with Kubrick," I said. "We can pick up with each other again after you finish *The Fugitive Kind*."

"Yeah, sure," Marlon said, smiling stiffly. "Give Kubrick my best."

Then he stepped into the shower stall and slammed the door so hard it almost shattered the glass.

After that, he began to avoid me on the set. I was no longer included in the story conferences, and after a take he didn't ask for my opinion. I was made to feel that I was in everyone's way, an intruder. I supposed that Marlon was angry with me for going with Kubrick. I thought he would soon get over it. After all, we'd had worse quarrels and been reconciled. But then, one day when I least expected it, Marlon fired me.

He was blocking the gun-dueling scene with Malden one morning. When it was set, the cameraman took over and Marlon came to me, took me aside, and said, "Freddie, I'm letting you go. I'm way over budget and I can't carry you anymore."

"*Carry* me? That's a hell of a way to put it."

[263]

"Take it any way you like," Marlon said, "but you're fired."

"As of when?"

"As of now."

"Don't you think there's a lot of hostility in the *way* you're firing me?"

"Mmmmm—nope. I don't feel any hostility toward you. As a matter of fact, I'm still going to give you that single-card screen credit I promised you. Your old Brooklyn buddies will be impressed when they see it."

The first assistant shouted, "Come on, Marlon, we're ready for you."

"Listen, Freddie, I can't stand around and bullshit with you. I've got work to do." And he hurried away to resume shooting.

At eight o'clock that night, my phone rang. It was Marlon. "Let's have dinner. Let's go to that Mexican joint with the waitress with the groovy ass."

"Let's skip dinners together for a while," I said.

Marlon seemed surprised. "Do you mean that?"

"Of course I do."

"Are you still pissed off about today?"

"I sure am."

"You'll get over it. We've had quarrels before and we've gotten over them. You'll get over this one too."

"Maybe."

"Come on, man, let's have a night on the town. After dinner we'll go to Strip City and look over those fine-looking strippers."

"I'm in no mood to see you tonight. Can't you understand that?"

"Okay, okay. See you around."

"Yeah," I said, and hung up.

Several weeks later I was awakened by a call at three o'clock in the morning.

"Did I wake you?" It was Marlon's tired voice.

"That's okay. What's up?"

"I'm down at Paramount, wearing out my eyeballs in the cutting room," he said. "I've been looking at film all day and night and I've lost my perspective on it. To coin a phrase, I can't see the forest for the trees. Why don't you come on down and give me a hand?"

"I'm in bed for the night," I said.

"Aw, come on, do me a favor and come down, will you?"

"Nope."

"You're a stubborn, hypersensitive, dumb Sicilian! And you're an ingrate." He slammed down the receiver.

It was another morning, a little later, and this time the call came at 4:00 A.M. I heard Marlon's voice, dim and blurred, saying, "How many Seconals have you ever taken at once?"

"What?"

"I said, how many Seconals have you ever taken at once?"

"Do you know what time it is? It's four A.M."

"So what? I've called at four before. Lots of times."

"Times have changed. Later . . ."

"Wait. Don't hang up. I want to talk to you."

I was fully awake by this time, and it suddenly occurred to me that he might have taken an overdose of sleeping pills.

"What did you say about Seconals?" I said.

"How many reds have you dropped at one time?"

"Two. Once I took four and I passed out for fourteen hours."

"Well, I've just taken six."

"Six! And you're still conscious?"

"Kinda."

"You're not trying to kill yourself, are you?"

"Of course not. You build up a tolerance for them real fast. Before you know it, you're dropping six just to get a little drowsy."

"I didn't know you were using barbiturates. How long has that been going on?"

"Years. On and off."

"That stuff is worse than heroin. In combination with alcohol, reds'll kill you. Sure as shootin'."

"I know. I know." Marlon's voice was growing dimmer.

"You're falling out," I said. "I'm going to hang up and you can get some sleep."

"No, no," he said, forcing himself awake. "Don't hang up. I want to talk."

For more than an hour, he rambled on and on incoherently. While he was talking he fell asleep without hanging up and I could hear his slow, heavy breathing.

Quietly, I hung up.

Not long after that, *One-Eyed Jacks* was finally released and proved to be a disappointment. It got split reviews and didn't draw at the box office. The blockbuster had turned out to be a dud. I had my own complaint, about the credit I was supposed to get. My title was assistant to the producer, but I wanted writing credit, not only because I had worked like hell on the script but because it meant much more to have that listing. To get a writing credit, however, it's necessary to prove to the Screen Writers' Guild that you have been responsible for a third of the film. I brought a suitcase to the Guild, filled with thousands of pages of script dating back to the *Burst of Vermilion* days. All that might be true, they said, but somebody somewhere at the studio didn't want to give me writing credit. I knew it could only have been Marlon. In the end, I did get my single-card credit, but as the lowly "assistant to the producer," another way of saying "gopher" (go-for).

What Paramount had done to Marlon was far worse. Sometimes professional film cutters are not as good as they think they are. They are inclined to think they know better, and after all Marlon's hard work in the cutting room, they had worked on it and completely cut out a subplot, a key scene in the picture. In it, Marlon rapes a Chinese girl while he is recuperating in a fishing village in Big Sur from the beating Malden has given him. He is learning to draw his gun again— symbolically, of course, getting back his balls. While he is practicing with the gun, he falls in love with the Chinese girl, who is a waitress in the local café. One rainy day he rapes her. This entire sequence was cut out, which led to a ridiculous situation in which Lisa Lu, the actress who played the girl, got screen credit as a featured player but her part had been cut to a bit.

In its rough cut, the film had run six hours, and it had been cut by two-thirds to get it in under two hours. All that was left was Brando. Whenever there had been any doubt on the set as to where to put the camera, the answer had been easy: "Keep it on the money, on Brando." The cutting had focused on him in the same manner and, in doing so, had lost everything he was trying to say. It was not Marlon's picture, but Paramount's.

After it opened, I went to Frank P. Rosenberg and asked him, "What do you do with the film you cut out of a picture like Marlon's?"

"Nothing. Throw it away, I guess," he said.

"After its first run," I suggested, "why not get the whole thing together, all six hours of it, and show it. A lot of people would like to see it."

"No, no." Frank P. Rosenberg shook his head. "It would be a very bad precedent—and it wouldn't be fair to the customers."

"There aren't many films you could do that with," I said.

"Forget it," he said curtly.

I still think a four- or five-hour version of *One-Eyed Jacks* wouldn't be half as dull as the two-hour version the public saw.

When I saw the movie for the first time, I left the theater feeling awful. All that time, money, and high hopes—wasted on a mediocre film. I wasn't surprised when *Esquire* Magazine administered the *coup de grâce*, awarding it the "Dubious Achievement of the Year—Brando on the Rocks."

It was over. The picture had ended, and so, I thought, had my long relationship with Marlon. But it didn't end as suddenly as that. We saw each other occasionally, and he got in the habit of calling me often, at two or three o'clock in the morning, his voice fogged with the pills he was taking. What he wanted me to do was listen while he talked himself to sleep, and out of the old habits of friendship I let him do it. His voice would mumble on and on, then slowly fade away until I could hear his regular breathing, after which I would hang up and go back to my own sleep.

I remember vividly two of the occasions I saw him, because they told me something more about the man I had known so long that I thought I knew everything about him.

He was living on Mulholland Drive in a Japanese-style house (an echo of *Sayonara*, perhaps), but Japanese or not, it had most of the features that Marlon always demanded of a house or an apartment. Its principal feature, as always, was the bedroom.

If Marlon had his way, and he usually did, the largest room anywhere he lived would always turn out to be the bed-

[268]

room. Whatever its original size, he would begin to stock it at once with books, records, scripts, *objets d'art*, coffee cups, milk-shake cups, and a wild conglomeration of things until it was so crowded that something had to be done. Then he would call in a set of carpenters, have a wall knocked out, and begin to expand. At the same time, he insisted that the bathroom must also be large. He wanted to be able to move around in it.

Marlon spent a great deal of time in his various bedrooms, and far from all of it was spent with women. Sometimes he would stay there alone for two or three days at a time, moody, thinking, reading, trying to relax. He read a great deal but seldom dipped into any fiction except for the scripts he was called upon to examine. These days, I understand, he is reading up on the life and hard times of the American Indian, but in those days he was deep into Zen, psychoanalysis, Rollo May, Karl Menninger, and Eric Hoffer, the self-proclaimed longshoreman-philosopher whose works Marlon liked so much he sent out dozens of copies to friends.

The bed itself was always king-size. Marlon moved around a lot in it, and sometimes he had to move a long way across its vast expanse to answer the telephone, which rang fairly constantly. He always heard the phone, no matter what else he might be doing, and he had it on a long cord so he could take it with him to the bathroom, or even to the nearby kitchen, so he wouldn't miss its ringing. To back that up, he had a pulsating light that announced an incoming call. Whenever possible, Marlon also liked to have a fireplace in the bedroom; the Mulholland Drive place had one.

Next to the bedroom, the most important room for Marlon was the kitchen, to which he made frequent trips because he had always been a compulsive eater. He reduced only at the time he was going to begin a picture, so that he could get into the costumes, but then while it was being made he would blow up until the buttons began to pop. He was so compulsive about it that often when we came to his house after having a big dinner out, his first act would be to rush to the refrigerator and begin prospecting. He loved grapefruit and ate dozens of them, but he also couldn't resist milk shakes or cheeseburgers. His favorite, however, was peanut-butter-and-jelly sandwiches, with milk, of which he could consume a quart with the practiced ease with which a confirmed alcoholic would toss down a drink.

Marlon made a few gestures in the direction of physical fitness. There were always some weights around in his bedroom—barbells and similar exercisers—but he seldom used them, and they gathered rust while he lay in bed, nude as usual, telling me he was going to get around to using them, or swearing yet again that he was going to go on a diet the next day.

Somehow, in the process of fooling himself about what he was doing, Marlon got his amphetamine habit and his diet-suppressing pills mixed up in his mind, so that he was using one to alibi for the other. I discovered this by accident one day. I knew that he had gotten into the deadly cycle of taking sleeping tablets at night, when he talked himself to sleep with me until the pills took effect, and amphetamines the following morning to get him through the day. Knowing as much as I did about drugs, I didn't have to be told he was on amphetamines. I recognized the signs—the tight-clenched jaw, the peculiar stare in the eyes, and the cords standing out in the neck.

While we were making *One-Eyed Jacks,* I had asked him point-blank one day, "Are you on uppers?" I had been watching him put his makeup on over his taut, tense jaws and along the bulging cords of his neck.

*Christian (Marlon's son by Anna Kashfi), Marlon's ex-wife
Movita, and his son by her, Miko.* (PHIL ROACH, PHOTOREPORTERS, INC.)

"No, of course not," he said defensively, "Why do you ask that?"

"Well, I just thought you might be."

"No. If you mean those pills you see me taking, those are diet depressants. I'm trying to lose some weight."

Later, alone in his dressing room, I saw the pills lying on a table, where he had carelessly left them, and decided to try one myself. I took a whole one with the coffee I was drinking, and in fifteen minutes I was floating above the set, higher than I had ever been, pressing against the ceiling. These were Marlon's "appetite suppressors"—and he was taking two or three of them at a time. I knew it must have been going on for a long time and his body had built up a resistance, or he would never have been able to do it.

But that was Marlon's life after *Jacks*, trying to pull himself together after its failure, appearing in one dismal picture after another, popping his pills, eating constantly, fighting the fat at the same time, and screwing. Somehow everything came together once more, including our relationship with each other and with girls, on the day four or five years after *Jacks* when he called and invited me to come over to the house on Mulholland Drive.

I arrived with a beautiful high-fashion model named Susan. Marquand was there, on a visit from France and staying with Marlon. He had been the "best friend" in France whenever Marlon was there, and now I could see he had superseded me, at least to some extent, as the Hollywood "best friend." And the scenario began unrolling as it always had as soon as Marlon saw my girl friend. Even more blatantly than he ever had in the past, he began at once to steal her. I supposed he thought that now I was no longer working for him, there was no particular need to make any pretense about it.

I could see that Susan wasn't particularly impressed by his attentions. As far as she was concerned, he was just another movie star, because she had already been the friend of Sam Spiegel, the producer, and of Yul Brynner. Susan knew her way around Hollywood.

Nevertheless, when she came into the room, Marlon gave her a long, admiring look, came over to her, and opened the coat she was wearing on this chilly night so that he could see her magnificent figure a little more clearly. She was model-thin and ordinarily would not have been his type (he liked a girl with more flesh), but Susan was an extremely sexy-looking girl. She permitted him to open her coat and stand there, seemingly transfixed by her remarkable body, which he took his time about examining. When I saw him do that, I knew he had every intention of embarrassing her, if he didn't succeed in screwing her, and of humiliating me once more at the same time.

While we sipped our drinks and nibbled at the cheese laid out for us, I watched him openly admiring her. In the middle of the small talk, he said suddenly, "Do you know, Sue, you remind me of my mother."

"For God's sake, Marlon," I said, "don't come on with that line of shit."

"No, no, I mean it," he said. "Wait a minute, and I'll show you."

He went into the bedroom and came back with a picture of Dodie. He was right. Except that Sue was a brunette and Dodie a blonde, she did look like Marlon's mother. Naturally, she was pleased and I think a little flattered.

Encouraged by this response, Marlon executed a maneuver that I knew to be one of his usual tricks; and although I had seen it happen a hundred times, I was drawn into it. Marquand took me over to a corner and engaged me in a meaningless conversation, something so philosophical I had to pay attention or go to sleep. While he was doing it, I saw out of the corner of my eye Marlon doing his disappearing act with Sue.

They were gone about ten minutes and then reappeared. I assumed he had been making arrangements with her. Marquand was still carrying on with me. By this time, he was showing me his small collection of exotic Oriental pipes designed for smoking hashish, and he had informed me that he had made some hashish jam by mixing it with marmalade. He went to the kitchen and got some out of the refrigerator, giving me a nice teaspoonful of it. I took it, knowing that when it is absorbed this way, it takes about an hour to hit.

Marlon was deep in conversation with Sue in another part of the room when Marquand inquired, "Has it hit you yet?"

"No," I said, "it hasn't, but I've got some pretty good grass with me and we could have some of it right now except I don't have any papers to roll it."

"That's no problem," Marquand said. "I've got some." He went into the bedroom and returned with some bamboo paper, giving it to me and appearing to expect me to roll the joints.

I hesitated. Marlon had always objected to pot, and as far as I knew, he still did. Was it possible he was using it now, along with the sleeping pills and the amphetamines? I could scarcely believe it, because back in New York he had often hesitated to come into my pad if he could smell the sweet odor of grass when the door was opened.

I could still remember, vividly, the only time I ever saw Marlon turn on. It was in the days when he was living at the Park Savoy with Maria, right after *Streetcar*, and I was living in the Village with Vicki, smoking grass and shooting up a little but not yet a junkie. I hadn't fooled Marlon about what I was doing.

"I always know when you're on something," he told me. "There's something that happens to your eyes."

When I told him what I was actually doing, his lively curiosity got the better of him for once.

"What does it do for you, this marijuana?" he wanted to know.

"Well, it makes you loose, so you enjoy sex, music, and conversation even more. It doesn't really do you any harm. It's really an anti-depressant."

"Just once I'd like to try some," Marlon said. "Why don't you get some and see if you can turn me on?"

I agreed, but I wanted to make sure he got high on this memorable occasion, so I waited until I heard some marvelous stuff from Brazil was available, so great they were calling it Golden Leaf. I plunged (it was very expensive) and bought an ounce, after which I hurried with it to Marlon's place.

"This is very great stuff," I told him "like vintage wine. I paid a hell of a lot for it, but I'm going to give you a quarter of an ounce."

"Okay," Marlon said. "When do we get high?"

"Tonight," I said. "Where?"

"Not here." Marlon looked around nervously. I guessed he was thinking of Maria. "We'll go somewhere else."

That night, in a friend's pad, we were ready; to my surprise, however, Marlon had brought Maria with him. I tamped some of the stuff into a lady's pipe and handed it to Marlon.

"Take deep drags," I instructed him. "Hold in the smoke as long as you can."

I'd taken only one puff of my own to realize how great the stuff *really* was. This stuff, I realized, was the kind that would get you high with two or three puffs. I glanced at Marlon, who had taken only his first one, and saw that he was absolutely stoned. I could see the change coming over his face, which was like a death mask, ashen pale. He grabbed my arm and hung on desperately.

"Take me home, Freddie," he said in a strange voice.

"What's the matter?" I asked him.

"Take me home," he repeated.

I laughed. "Don't worry. You're only on marijuana."

"Don't laugh," Marlon said almost desperately. "Take me home."

I recognized the symptoms. He had "panicked out," as they say of someone who gets stoned for the first time and becomes frightened because he loses control.

"Okay," I said, trying to reassure him. "Maybe I gave you a little too much. Come on."

[275]

While he clung to me, I got him out to a cab and took him home. "Are you all right now, man?" I asked him.

"Yes, I'm okay now. It's all right," he said.

I realized that Marlon, who hated to lose control of himself, had probably panicked worse than the usual novice, and, thinking he might still be curious, I left some pot with him.

A few days later, having smoked my own supply and remembering what I'd given him, I went up to the Park Savoy to see if there might be any left.

"Are you smoking any of what I gave you that night?" I inquired.

Maria, who was with him, interrupted. "I took the stuff and flushed it down the toilet," she told me angrily.

I was almost ill at the thought of that beautiful Golden Leaf floating down the sewer system.

"For God's sake, why? Why didn't you give it to me if you wanted to get rid of it."

Maria put on her prim, self-righteous look. "Because I don't approve of it," she said.

Marlon had little to say. I understood now that he hadn't been loose enough to take that kind of stuff. In those days he was in a constant state of panic without taking anything, although he never showed it. Kazan had persuaded him to go to a psychiatrist, a man who had written a book titled *Neurotics, Curable and Incurable*. Meeting Marlon one day on his way to the doctor's office, I went with him, at his earnest request. While I was waiting for him, I observed that all the furniture in the waiting room was nailed to the floor. Everything, that is, except a brass ashtray, and when I discovered it was loose, I stole it.

As we left, I said to Marlon, "I'm a little ashamed, but I couldn't help it. I stole something from your shrink," and I showed him what it was.

"Give it to me," Marlon said sternly, and I did. Later he took it back and, as he told me, had a talk with the doctor about his friend (me), a junkie who refused to see a psychiatrist.

"If he won't do that," the doctor said positively, "he hasn't got a Chinaman's chance in life." I thought it was rather an odd way for a psychiatrist to talk.

All these memories flashed through my mind as I hesitated before Marquand that night in the house on Mulholland Drive, wondering if Marlon had really changed in his attitude about drugs.

"Shall I roll it here?" I asked Marquand doubtfully. "Marlon might object."

"Why don't you do it in the john?" Marquand said smoothly.

While I was rolling the joint in the bathroom, it occurred to me that this was probably just another ploy Marquand was using so that Marlon could be alone with Sue. While I was meditating morosely on this probability, rolling the joint meanwhile, the door flew open and there stood Marlon. He jerked the joint out of my hand, threw it in the bowl, and flushed it away.

"Now why in the hell did you do that?" I asked in exasperation.

"Because I don't want that stuff in my house," he said.

"You didn't have to flush it down the toilet. I would have carried it away with me."

"I just don't want it here."

I saw Marquand standing behind him. Obviously, he had betrayed me. I couldn't understand the whole thing. If Marlon hated grass so much, what was he doing having Marquand as his house guest—a man who kept hashish jam in the refrigerator, who smoked himself, and who in fact had once almost

Christian, en route to court with his father.
(WIDE WORLD PHOTOS)

been busted in London, a fact Marlon knew as well as I did. It was even more mystifying when I learned later that Marlon had been smoking both pot and hashish with Marquand. For the moment, however, it was puzzling enough that Marlon wasn't going to let me have one lousy joint in his house.

"Why not?" I asked him. "When I was on junk, I used to carry my works into your place, and you knew I had them on me, and you didn't say anything. Why now?"

Marlon's voice was tight. "Don't you know I'm fighting for the custody of my son? Anna is down there telling the judge that Christian belongs with her because this isn't a healthy place for him to be, with my unsavory friends and the bad company I keep. Do you know who the bad people are, Freddie? One of them is you—a junkie, a shoplifter."

"Maybe that was true once. Of course it was true. You know it. But that was a long time ago, and I've reformed. What's the matter with you anyway, Marlon? Are you going to be acting out some role when you get on the witness stand? If you do, you'll lose that custody fight sure as hell."

Marlon looked at me for a moment, his face dark, his eyes hard. I could see that he was in a rage. Turning on his heel, he rushed out and into the kitchen. Marquand followed him, returning in a moment to tell me, "Marlon's really in a rage. He told me he had to leave because he didn't want to punch you in the nose."

"Let him try it," I said, "and I'll make him look like a character actor so the only job he'll be able to get will be in a horror movie."

I went back into the living room, and before long Marlon joined us. He had cooled down and was civil enough to me. Soon afterward, I took Sue home. As we were driving along, she said, "Why do you keep on seeing Marlon? He's so hostile to you, so competitive."

"Something has gone wrong with him," I said, "and I don't know what it is. But I keep seeing him because I still love the guy. That's why."

Something had changed that night, however, and we were farther apart than before. He rarely called me. Maybe he didn't want to risk losing the custody fight, I thought, by associating with me, and, if so, I could understand that.

Nearly a half year went by, and Christmas was approaching. I was hearing from Marlon a little more frequently, but mostly they were his foggy 3:00 A.M. calls, when he was talking himself to sleep. But then one day, only a week before Christmas, he called during the day and said, as though nothing had ever happened, "Why don't you come up and help us decorate the tree? Marquand's here and a pretty little Japanese chick."

"I'm not alone," I said, "and I know you don't like to have strangers around."

"Who's with you?"

I told him. A friend had called me from New York and said, "Listen, do me a favor. This girl I know is coming out to Hollywood for a few days. She doesn't know anybody there, and I thought maybe you'd show her around." I agreed without much enthusiasm, because it was like the old-fashioned blind date. I had gone to the Roosevelt Hotel, where the girl was to stay, and called her from the lobby. She said she'd be right down, and when she stepped out of the elevator I could have kissed my New York friend. She was black and beautiful, marvelous in every respect. It was all downhill from her first warm greeting, "Are you Carlo?" In no time at all we had gone out to dinner, talked through a long evening, and come back to my place, where we went right to bed.

Later that night I said to her, "Why don't you stay here with me? It'll be a lot more fun than the Roosevelt."

"I thought you'd never ask," she said.

She kept her room at the hotel (insurance, maybe?) but moved in with me.

All this I told Marlon, but he stopped listening right after I finished describing the girl. "Bring her up," he said.

"I thought you didn't like strangers around," I said.

"Don't be silly," Marlon told me. "Bring her."

When I hung up, I said to the girl—I'll call her Linda—"We've been invited to come and help a friend of mine trim his Christmas tree. Do you want to come?"

"Of course," Linda said. "That would be lovely."

"The friend's name is Marlon Brando," I told her.

She tried to conceal her sheer delight at this news, but I could tell she was excited and pleased. Ahead of me, I could see the familiar scenario unfolding again.

When Linda appeared, ready to go, I was sure of it. She wore an electric orange pants suit, with the upper part cut so low her delectable breasts were nearly falling out. She looked superb, and I knew Marlon would go out of his mind when he saw her.

But I hadn't counted on the effect she would have on Marquand. Maybe he thought I only went around with high-class whores, but when we came into the living room, he assumed he could take the liberty of walking up to Linda, opening her decolletage even wider, peering down in, and then reaching inside to feel her breast.

If I hadn't been prepared, Linda was. She took a short step back from him to get a better angle and swung a haymaker from the floor that almost took his head off. He staggered and nearly fell over. The Christmas party was off to a great start, I thought.

At that moment, Marlon walked in from the bedroom. He didn't appear to notice what had happened to Marquand, but came straight over to Linda, and, as I had expected, demonstrated in every possible way that he was completely taken with her.

Then, as though the cameras had started to roll on order, a scene began to develop that was exactly like the one with Sue six months before. Having anticipated it, however, I had tried to protect myself. On the way to Marlon's house, I had told Linda, "Marlon's going to come on in a big way with you. If you want to fuck him, okay, but I'm asking you to do it later. Please don't embarrass me."

"What kind of girl do you think I am?" she had said. "Of course I wouldn't do anything like that. I'm coming to the party with you, and I'll leave with you."

That was before she saw Marlon. They hadn't talked long before Marquand went into his routine, taking me aside for an earnest conversation while Linda and Marlon disappeared. I should have known better, but I wasn't worried this time because of Linda's reassurance.

When they came back, Marlon signaled me to come over to him while Marquand was taking Linda aside, apologizing profusely to her for his earlier actions.

"Come into the bedroom with me," Marlon said.

Here it comes, I thought. He's going to tell me that Linda's staying with him. Instead, he said, "Lie down on the floor, flat on your stomach."

"What's this all about? What for?" I inquired, doing what he asked.

"Because I want to arm-wrestle with you," he said, stretching out on his stomach on the floor, but facing me so our right arms could come together.

"Now why do you want to do this?" I asked him. "I know you can beat me. You've done it a thousand times. You've proved you're far stronger than I am. Why do it again?"

[282]

"Oh, come on, Freddie. It's fun."

We wrestled and he beat me, of course, quickly bending my arm far over until my knuckles hit the floor. Then he gave me different kinds of advantage and still beat me every time. What is this all about? I kept wondering.

"Okay," I said at last, "you beat me. Now let's go back and join the others."

Abruptly, Marlon said, "Do me a favor, Freddie, and leave that girl with me."

"No," I said. "This time I'm not going to do it."

"Come on," he tried to cajole me. "You've got a lot of other girls. And besides, you've done this for me a thousand times before."

"I know I have, but I'm not working for you anymore, and I don't feel the same way. This girl is only going to be here for a couple of days. I've been having a great time with her in bed, and I want her, for the rest of the time she's going to be in town."

Marlon leaned back and looked at me narrowly.

"Well, she's going to stay anyway," he said.

"What makes you think she is?"

"I asked her if she would, and she agreed. That's why."

"I don't believe it."

"Do you want her to come in here and tell you herself?"

"Yes, I do."

He called her in and said, "Linda, tell Freddie that it's true you agreed to stay here with me tonight."

Linda was nervous, but she looked me right in the eye.

"I'm going to stay here tonight with Marlon," she said.

With that, I completely lost my temper for once. Maybe I shouldn't say "for once." Sicilians aren't particularly well known for their restraint. But I had never been so angry with

Marlon, and, for that matter, I was as angry with Linda for her betrayal.

"You've always been hostile to me," I told Marlon, "particularly in situations like this. You've at least tried to cover it up before, but I don't know how it could be more blatant now. I can't believe it, but it seems to me you'd do anything to hurt me. Why do you want me to go through this kind of humiliation, anyway? What is it with you, Marlon? You're always making such a pretense of being kind to people, but the fact of the matter is that you murder them when you get a chance. I could have taken Linda home, and you could have made arrangements to see her some other time, even later tonight. I told her she could do that, if she wanted to. But you had to do it this way, to humiliate me in front of her."

Marlon gave me that same narrow look, and said in a level voice, "Freddie, do you want to argue with me about whether she's your girl or anybody's?"

"Yes, I do," I said.

"Okay," he said, and asked Linda to wait for us in the living room. After he shut the door, he and Christian and I sprawled out on Marlon's king-size bed and went on with the argument. Marlon began by reminding me of a long-forgotten episode when another guy had complained that I had taken his girl away from him, and I had laughed about it.

"I don't do things like that," I said. "That girl told me she'd broken up with the other guy. She said he was still calling her up and bothering her and trying to get back with her again, but she wouldn't have any part of it. She told me she was free, and she wanted to have a date with me."

"That isn't the way I remember it," Marlon said. "I remember that her boy friend confronted you and accused you of stealing his girl."

[285]

"That's right, he did, and I told him, 'If she's your girl, what's she doing having a date with me? I don't have any claim on her.' Besides, there's such a thing as observing the social amenities. It's all that hostility of yours I object to. If Linda prefers you, I might be hurt, but okay—just spare me the kind of humiliation you gave me tonight."

The argument went on for about an hour. Marquand joined in from time to time, always agreeing with Marlon, of course, because he was constantly trying to curry favor, and asserting that a girl was the property of whatever man she happened to be with at the time. It was a lucky thing Gloria Steinem wasn't a member of that group.

"I'm not going to argue anymore," I said at last. "You're both pricks as far as I'm concerned."

Marquand got up and looked out through the bedroom door. Beyond him we could see Linda, pacing up and down in the living room, biting her nails, obviously wondering what on earth had been going on in the bedroom for a whole hour.

"If you really had the hots for her," I said to Marlon, "you'd be screwing her by this time instead of arguing with me."

He didn't answer, and shortly after that I left. Marlon was right. Linda didn't come back that night. In the early morning she went to the Roosevelt, where she had kept her insurance room, and called me about nine o'clock, in tears, trying to apologize for hurting me.

"It's too late for that," I told her. "I don't care. If that's the kind of a girl you are, I don't want to see you again."

Her voice was pleading. "Listen, I've got to get out to the airport and catch my plane back to New York, and I'm stuck. I haven't got a car and I don't have enough for the cab fare. Wouldn't you please, please drive me out and let me explain to you on the way?"

There was a little more argument, then reluctantly I gave in.

As we drove out to the airport, she described her evening with Marlon. "We went to bed all right," she said, "but then he began to talk, and we talked until it was almost morning. I kept wondering and wondering when he was going to make love to me, but he just went on talking. Finally the sun was coming up and I could feel my eyes closing, and then right in the middle of a sentence he stopped talking and I could see he was asleep. So there I was, propped up on one elbow, watching this famous movie star sleeping like a corpse, lying on his back and beginning to snore. It was too much. I got up and dressed and left and went back to the hotel. He never touched me, Carlo."

I didn't really believe her. It sounded like a story Marlon had made up and instructed her to tell me, with the idea that it would cool me off. I told her I didn't believe it.

"But I swear to God," she said fervently, "on everything that's holy—Marlon never screwed me."

I let myself believe it was true and cooled off. Linda went back to New York, but it wasn't the end of her affair with Marlon by any means. She was quite frank about it. Every now and then she would call me and tell me how Marlon had called her whenever he came to New York, and taken her to lunch and the theater; and although she didn't say so, I presumed he also screwed her. He even took her down to his island in the South Pacific, where he fled from time to time. They were on the island when the inevitable moment came, as it always did, that Marlon decided she would have to go. He did it in his usual way, beginning by neglecting her and going off screwing with other girls, making no particular attempt to hide it, so that she was alone and frustrated a good part of the time. Naturally, she looked for a little action of her own

and wound up screwing a Tahitian man. Marlon found out about it and used it as an excuse to kick her out, ordering her to leave the island at once. He never spoke to her again.

After the episode with Linda, I saw Marlon with increasing infrequency. Our long relationship seemed to be ending, not in a burst of recrimination, like the argument over Linda, but simply dwindling away. Too much had come between us. After *Laughter in the Dark,* there was no work for me in Hollywood, and I was getting nowhere fast, so I went back to New York.

Within a couple of years I found myself getting hooked on junk again, but this time I had sense enough, or will power enough, or whatever, to shake the habit off before it was too late. Then I had a nervous breakdown and had to check in at the hospital. Marlon came into town while I was there and somehow found me, as he always seemed to be able to do. He asked me to attend the premiere of *Mutiny on the Bounty* with him, and I said I'd be glad to, but I never showed up. He called the hospital again and asked me to come see him at the Plaza. I got a pass and visited him. We drank and talked and pretty soon he said, "Is there anything I can do for you, Freddie? Anything?"

"No, nothing," I said.

When I last saw Marlon, it was Christmastime 1968. He had been working on the movie called *Burn!* and had taken time off to come home, very dissatisfied with the way the picture was going.

I had been drinking tea with James Baldwin one afternoon at his place when Marlon called, not knowing I was there. After working on the scenario of a biography of Malcolm X, Jimmy was talking with me about our possible collaboration on a screenplay for a movie that Al Ruddy, the producer, wanted to do, called *The Pimp,* based on the life of a well-

[289]

known flesh entrepreneur named Iceberg Slim. The production never got off the ground, and Ruddy later became the producer of *The Godfather*.

While we were talking about this project, the phone rang. I could hear Jimmy going on with someone, and then I heard him say, "There's a friend of yours here. Who? It's Carlo Fiore." A pause, then, "Yes, I'll put him on."

"It's your friend, Marlon," Jimmy said, returning. "He wants to talk to you."

I hadn't seen Marlon or talked with him for quite some time, but his familiar voice was as cordial as ever. We chatted a little about unimportant things, and finally Marlon said, "Why don't you and Jimmy come over tomorrow and have dinner?"

I agreed, and the next day we arrived at Brando's home in what might be called holiday high spirits. I brought a blonde beauty with me named Diane, an aspiring movie star. Marlon welcomed us all with what seemed genuine pleasure. There were old friends there—Wally Cox, his wife, their sixteen-year-old daughter, and Christian Marquand. Wally seemed terribly depressed, his wife determinedly cheerful, and his daughter shy. Marquand, who was then working on a de-layed movie bomb called *Candy*, was playing his usual role of French charmer.

Seeing Marlon was the real shocker. He was wearing a poncho, one of those shapeless slipover robes common south of the border. His hair was very long and getting quite gray, like his mustache and small beard. The poncho covered him com-pletely, making him look fat, but it was impossible to tell whether he was or not.

The talk flowed on, but there was something missing. Mar-lon seemed to be there, yet not there. He looked like a man who was chronically saddened. I realized that it was the first time we had ever been together when we neither laughed nor got angry with each other.

"Why don't you take off that poncho?" I asked him. "It's very warm in here. How can you stand it, sitting beside that fireplace?"

"Why should I take it off?" Marlon said.

"Because I can't see your body, and so I can't tell what shape you're in."

"If that's all you want, I'll show you," Marlon said.

Like a girl, he pulled up the poncho, taking his shirt along with it. For the first time I could see that he had gotten fat and flabby. I couldn't think of anything that would be safe to say and changed the subject.

"How is it, working with Pontecorvo?"

"All right. Pretty good, I guess."

"How is he at directing actors?"

Marlon's face clouded. "Not so good—not for me, at least. I don't like what he's doing."

The party went on, and finally Marlon, Jimmy, and I were lying on the floor in front of the fireplace, talking. I was surprised that Marlon hadn't come on with Diane, as he always had with my girls, but he was no more than polite to her.

Baldwin talked about people in the civil-rights movement, remarking that Malcolm's wife had not been at all the kind of woman he had expected her to be.

"Aren't you active in the movement anymore?" I asked Marlon. "I haven't heard about you doing anything lately."

"Blacks don't want whites to be anything but foot soldiers these days," Marlon answered somberly.

If that was true, it explained his noninvolvement; he would never cast himself as a foot soldier. I wondered later if his new cause, that of the American Indian, had come about because he thought that the Indians needed white generals.

We talked a little longer, but the conversation trailed off. Baldwin seemed to be obviously disappointed in the quality of the talk with Marlon, and so was I, although perhaps for different reasons. We left a little while later. Ironically, I didn't take Diane with me, but without any request from Marlon. She didn't want to leave, and since she wasn't my girl and I had no special interest in her, I had no objection. Jimmy and I went back to his place and talked of other things.

Marlon called next morning. "What did you think of Baldwin?" he wanted to know.

"I think he's beautiful," I said.

"Well, I don't know. Some of the other black activists I talk to seem to think he's becoming a Tom."

"They've got a nerve. Baldwin's opened plenty of doors for a lot of those guys. They ought to be grateful instead of putting him down."

"Well, maybe . . ."

"No maybe about it. He's done a hell of a lot for the whole movement."

Marlon agreed and changed the subject. He asked me what I was going to do next. As for himself, he said, he was thinking about retiring. I had heard that a dozen times before, but I knew he couldn't afford it. He had made a lot of money, true, but he was also helping to support three households besides his own—Anna Kashfi and his son, Movita and another son, Tarita (a Tahitian beauty he had met while making *Mutiny on the Bounty*) and their son and daughter, besides gifts to his sister Franny, who was married and living in Nebraska. Not to mention his sister Jocelyn. It is not an uncommon movie-star problem.

After that joyless dinner party, I didn't hear from Marlon again until the day of Martin Luther King's assassination, when he called to commiserate about the tragedy. We talked

for a while about what had happened, then that conversation petered out too. I haven't heard from him since.

No star except Marlon could have survived the extraordinary string of straight bombs he appeared in. But after twelve bad movies and ten years of waiting, he scored his greatest motion-picture success in *The Godfather* and followed it with *Last Tango in Paris*. As *The Godfather* demonstrated, his talent was always there; it hadn't diminished. He only needed a good picture. Now he has come back to claim his rightful title as the world's foremost actor.

I wish him well. I really do.